DISCIPLE *for* LIFE

Extraordinary

ORDINARY PEOPLE. EXTRAORDINARY GOD.

Darrin Patrick

Adapted for small groups by Stephen Hess

LifeWay Press®
Nashville, Tennessee

MW01127639

Published by LifeWay Press® • © 2016 Darrin Patrick

No part of this book may be reproduced or transmitted in any form or by any means, electronic or mechanical, including photocopying and recording, or by any information storage or retrieval system, except as may be expressly permitted in writing by the publisher. Requests for permission should be addressed in writing to LifeWay Press®; One LifeWay Plaza; Nashville, TN 37234-0152.

ISBN 978-1-4300-5510-5 • Item 006104040

Dewey decimal classification: 221.92

Subject headings: BIBLE. O.T.--BIOGRAPHY / GOD-WILL / BIBLE. O.T.—HISTORY OF BIBLICAL EVENTS

Unless otherwise noted, Scripture quotations are taken from the The Holy Bible, English Standard Version® (ESV®) copyright © 2001 by Crossway, a publishing ministry of Good News Publishers. Used by permission. All rights reserved. Scripture quotations marked HCSB are from the Holman Christian Standard Bible®, copyright 1999, 2000, 2002, 2003, 2009 by Holman Bible Publishers. Used by permission.

To order additional copies of this resource, write to LifeWay Christian Resources Customer Service; One LifeWay Plaza; Nashville, TN 37234-0113; fax 615.251.5933; phone toll free 800.458.2772; order online at www.lifeway.com; email orderentry@lifeway.com; or visit the LifeWay Christian Store serving you.

Printed in the United States of America

Groups Ministry Publishing • LifeWay Resources

One LifeWay Plaza • Nashville, TN 37234-0152

Contents

About Darrin Patrick

Darrin founded The Journey in 2002 in the urban core of St. Louis, Missouri. The Journey has six locations and has released seven church plants. Darrin is Vice President of the Acts 29 Church Planting Network and has helped start multiple non-profits in St. Louis. He also serves as Chaplain to the St. Louis Cardinals.

After earning his Bachelor of Arts in Biblical Languages from Southwest Baptist University and a Master's of Divinity (summa cum laude) from Midwestern Baptist Theological Seminary, Darrin earned his Doctor of Ministry from Covenant Seminary. Darrin is author of *The Dude's Guide to Manhood, Church Planter,* co-author of *Replant* and *For the City,* and contributor to the *ESV Gospel Transformation Bible* and *Don't Call It a Comeback.* He and his wife, Amie, recently released their first book, entitled, *The Dude's Guide to Marriage.*

Darrin is married to his high school sweetheart, Amie, and they have four beautiful children: Glory, Grace, Drew, and Delainey.

You can find more from Darrin and follow him at:

Blog/Resources – *DarrinPatrick.org*

Twitter - @DarrinPatrick

Facebook.com/DarrinPatrick

Instagram.com/drdarrinpatrick

TheDudesGuide.org

Introduction

If we're honest, many of us have drifted to a place of boredom or even cynicism spiritually. Our lives seem plain and ordinary. Not only do we recognize that we're not perfect, sometimes we're painfully aware of past or current struggles. But deep down we have a longing for something more, something extraordinary.

The real question in all of our hearts,
whether we know it or not, is:
CAN GOD USE ME?

The good news is that God is not asking us to be extraordinary. He's asking us to point to the One who is extraordinary—Jesus. In Scripture we see that God is in the business of taking flawed men and women to do things through them that they never could have imagined.

Over the next six weeks, we'll look at the lives of:

Adam who was tempted to be extraordinary without God.
Abraham who responded to God's call to leave an extraordinary legacy.
Moses who experienced extraordinary power yet wrestled with self-doubt.
Joshua who was given the extraordinary responsibility of leadership.
Job who trusted God without ever understanding his extraordinary suffering.
Esther who revealed God's extraordinary sovereignty in ordinary decisions.

My prayer is that we'll clearly see that these people were ordinary. God is extraordinary. We'll see that God invites us in our normal everyday lives to leave our boredom and cynicism aside to join His extraordinary mission.

How to Use This Study

This Bible study book includes six weeks of content. Each week has an introductory page summarizing the focus of study, followed by content designed for groups and for individuals.

GROUP SESSIONS

Regardless of what day of the week your group meets, each week of content begins with the group session. This group session is designed to be one hour or more—with approximately 15 minutes of teaching and 45 minutes of personal interaction. It's even better if your group is able to meet longer than an hour, allowing more time for participants to interact with one another.

Each group session uses the following format to facilitate simple yet meaningful interaction among group members, with God's Word, and with the video teaching by Darrin Patrick.

Start

This page includes questions to get the conversation started, to review the previous week's practical application, and to introduce the video segment.

Watch

This page includes key points from Darrin Patrick's teaching, along with blanks for taking notes as participants watch the video.

Discuss

These two pages include questions and statements that guide the group to respond to the video teaching and to relevant Bible passages.

Pray

This final page of each group session includes a prompt for your closing time of prayer together and space for recording prayer requests of group members.

INDIVIDUAL DISCOVERY

Each of the *Disciple for Life* small-group resources also provides individuals with optional activities during the week, appealing to different learning styles, schedules, and levels of engagement. These options include a plan for application and accountability, a Scripture reading plan with journaling prompts, a devotional, and two personal studies.

This Week's Plan

Immediately following the group session's prayer page is a weekly plan for everyone to engage with that week's focal point, regardless of a person's maturity level or that week's schedule.

You can choose to take advantage of some or all of the options provided. Those options are divided into three categories.

Read

A daily reading plan is outlined for Scriptures related to the group session. Space for personal notes is also provided. Information about how to use the HEAR journaling method for reading Scripture can be found on pages 8-11.

Reflect

A one-page devotional option is provided each week to help you reflect on a biblical truth related to the group session.

Personal Study

Two personal studies are provided each week to take individuals deeper into Scripture and to supplement the biblical truths introduced in the teaching time. These pages challenge individuals to grow in their understanding of God's Word and to identify practical application in their own lives.

LEADER GUIDES

Pages 120-131 in the back of this book contain a guide to develop a leader's understanding of the thought process behind questions and how to engage group members at different levels in life-changing discussion.

The *HEAR* Journaling Method for Reading Scripture

Daily Bible Reading

Disciple for Life small-group Bible studies include a daily reading plan for each week. Making time in a busy schedule to focus on God through His Word is a vital part of the Christian life. If you're unable to do anything else provided in your book during a certain week, try to spend a few minutes in God's Word. The verse selections will take you deeper into stories and concepts related to the teaching and discussion during that week's group session.

Why Do You Need a Plan?

When you're a new believer, or at various times in your life, you may find yourself in a place where you don't know where to begin reading your Bible or how to personally approach Scripture. You may have tried the open-and-point method where you simply open your Bible and point to a verse, hoping to get something out of the random selection from God's Word. Reading random Scriptures will not provide solid biblical growth any more then eating random food out of you pantry will provide solid physical growth.

An effective plan must be well-balanced for healthy growth. When it comes to reading the Bible, well-balanced and effective means reading and applying. A regular habit is great, but it's not enough to simply check a box off your task list when you've completed your daily reading. Knowing more about God is also great, but it's still not enough to read simply for spiritual knowledge. You also want to respond to what you are reading by taking action as you listen to what God is saying. After all, it's God's Word.

In order to digest more of the Word, *Disciple for Life* small-group Bible studies not only provide a weekly reading plan, but also encourage you to use a simplified version of the HEAR journaling method. (If this method proves to be helpful in your personal growth, check out *Foundations: A 260-Day Bible Reading Plan for Busy Believers* by Robby and Kandi Gallaty.)

Journaling What You HEAR in God's Word

You may or may not choose to keep a separate journal in addition to the space provided in this book. A separate journal would provide extra space as well as the opportunity to continue your journal after this study is completed. The HEAR journaling method promotes reading the Bible with a life-transforming purpose. You will be reading in order to understand and respond to God's Word.

The HEAR acronym stands for Highlight, Explain, Apply, and Respond. Each of these four steps contributes to creating an atmosphere to hear God speak. After settling on a reading plan (like the one provided in this book for each week), establish a time for studying God's Word. Then you will be ready to HEAR from God.

Before You Begin–The Most Important Step

To really HEAR God speak to you through His Word, you always need to begin your time with prayer. Pause and sincerely ask God to speak to you. It may seem trite, but it's absolutely imperative that we seek God's guidance in order to understand His Word (see 1 Cor. 2:12-14). Every time you open your Bible, pray a simple prayer like the one David prayed: "Open my eyes so that I may contemplate wonderful things from Your instruction" (Ps. 119:18).

H = Highlight

After praying for the Holy Spirit's guidance, open your book to the week's Reading Plan, open a journal if you'd like more space than what's provided in this book, and open your Bible. For an illustration, let's assume you are reading Philippians 4:10-13. Verse 13 may really jump out and speak to you as something you want to remember. In your Bible, you would simply highlight Philippians 4:13.

If keeping a HEAR journal, on the top line write the Scripture reference, the date, and make up a title to summarize the meaning of the passage. Then write the letter "H" and write out the verse that stood out and that you highlighted in your Bible. This practice will make it easy to look back through your journal to find a passage you want to revisit in the future.

E = Explain

After you have highlighted your verse(s), you will want to explain what the text means. Most simply, how would you summarize this passage in your own words? By asking some simple questions, with the help of God's Spirit, you can understand the meaning of the passage or verse. (A good study Bible can help you with answers to more in-depth questions as you learn to explain a passage of Scripture.) Here are a few good questions to get you started:

- Why was it written?

- To whom was it originally written?

- How does the passage fit with the verses before and after it?

- Why would the Holy Spirit include this passage in the book?

- What is God intending to communicate through the text?

If keeping a HEAR journal, below the "H," write the letter "E" and explain the text in your own words. Record any answers to questions that help you understand the passage of Scripture.

A = Apply

At this point, you are beginning the process of discovering the specific and personal word that God has for you from His Word. What is important is that you are engaging the text and wrestling with the meaning. Application is the heart of the process. Everything you have done so far culminates under this heading. As you have done before, answer a series of questions to uncover the significance of these verses to you personally, questions like:

- How can this help me?

- What is God saying to me?

- What would the application of this verse look like in my life?

These questions bridge the gap between the ancient world and your world today. They provide a way for God to speak to you through the specific passage or verse.

If keeping a HEAR journal, write the letter "A" under the letter "E" where you wrote a short summary explaining the text. Challenge yourself to write between two and five sentences about how the text applies to your life.

R = Respond

Finally, you will respond to the text. A personal response may take on many forms. You may write an action step to do, describe a change in perspective, or simply respond in prayer to what you've learned. For example, you may ask for help being bold or generous, you may need to repent of unconfessed sin, or you may need to praise God. Keep in mind that this is a response to what you have just read.

In this book (if you're not keeping a journal), write your personal application and response in the space provided with each passage of Scripture. You may want to write a brief explanation and application summary. *The verse means this, so I can or will do this...*

If keeping a HEAR journal, write the letter "R" along with how you will Respond to what you Highlighted, Explained, and Applied.

Notice that all of the words in the HEAR method are action words: Highlight, Explain, Apply, Respond. God doesn't want us to sit back and wait for Him to drop some truth into our laps. Instead of waiting passively, God desires that we actively pursue Him. Jesus said:

> "Keep asking, and it will be given to you. Keep searching, and you
> will find. Keep knocking, and the door will be opened to you."
> Matt. 7:7, HCSB

Adam

Week 1

Adam and Eve were placed into a world that was perfectly designed for them to connect with God. This first man and woman were unique among all of creation as God's image-bearers (see Gen. 1:26-27). Walking in the garden in the cool of the day, they experienced an extraordinary relationship with God. They were called to rule over God's creation in God's name for God's glory.

As they honored God as Creator and ultimate authority, they were free to enjoy His creation. But everything changed after being offered a taste of life apart from God. Satan tempted Adam and Eve with the opportunity to be "like God" (Gen. 3:5). Though they were already created in God's "likeness" (Gen. 1:26), they gave into forbidden fruit and tasted death. Life as they knew it spiraled downward in what we call: the fall of man.

They believed lies about God and themselves.

Sin entered the world.

Shame entered their hearts.

They hid.

Now, we all do the same.

So the Creator entered His creation. Our only hope is in Jesus—God become man—who tasted death for us so that we may experience life through faith. The Word of God offers us the wisdom we now need to overcome temptation and walk in freedom by the power of the Holy Spirit.

Start

Welcome everyone to the first group session.

Use the following content to start your time together.

In the last few years, superheroes have made a dramatic comeback to the big screen. Marvel seems to put out a summer blockbuster each year. Even biblical stories have been turned into heroic adventures—using creative license—with Darren Aronofsky's *Noah* and Ridley Scott's *Exodus: God and Kings*.

> **What is it about heroes and epic stories that captures our imagination?**

These stories invite us to imagine the extraordinary. Deep down, we want to be extraordinary ourselves, not just witness it around us. We don't want to just behold the heroic, we want to *be* heroic.

In these next six weeks, we want to unearth that buried desire for more. We want to learn how each of us can be used by God to do extraordinary things. Each week we'll spotlight a so-called hero in the Old Testament to see how he or she was a truly ordinary person with an extraordinary and powerful God.

Let's see what Darrin has to say in video session 1 about God's original plan for mankind at the beginning of the story, right there in the first few pages of the Bible.

Pray for God to open your hearts and minds before showing the video for session 1.

Watch

Use the space below to follow along and take notes as you watch video session 1.

Paradise wasn't paradise without _____.

Paradise wasn't paradise without _____.

We have a desire to bring _____ out of _____.

Anytime a person doesn't follow the _____ of God, it's because they're following a _____ of Satan.

Satan tempts us with the offer of becoming _____ apart from God.

Though we fail to _____ to God in our sin, God _____ to us in our sin.

Scriptures: Genesis 1-3

Discuss

Use the statements and questions below to discuss the video.

Darrin explained that we were created for an extraordinary relationship *with* God and given extraordinary responsibility *from* God.

> **How does this affect your view of God? Of yourself? Of others?**

Being made "in the image of God" (Gen. 1:27) means that we have been designed to reflect God's character in this world.

> **What comes to mind when you think of God's character?**

> **What about God's character is most meaningful to you?**

> **Which parts of God's character are hardest for you to reflect? Why?**

Darrin identified our work as one way we reflect God's image. He defines work (stewardship) as bringing order out of chaos.

> **Where do you see chaos in the world? In your own life?**

> **How do you seek to bring order out of chaos in these areas of life? In your work? In your home?**

> **How does knowing that God made you a steward of His creation transform the way you approach relationships and responsibilities?**

In Genesis 3 we see chaos enter our lives as relationships and responsibilities are neglected. Let's look at the words of the serpent (Satan):

Read aloud Genesis 3:1-6.

> **How did the serpent tempt Eve?**

> **What can you learn from Adam and Eve's passivity toward sin?**

> **Temptation is always a lie. What are some specific examples of how temptation promises something extraordinary apart from God?**

Read aloud Genesis 3:7-13.

What does this reveal about God? About the consequences of sin?

In an effort that's tragic but almost comical in its absurdity, Adam and Eve try to hide from God. Then Adam has the audacity to blame Eve (and God for making Eve) for his sin. Eve then blames the serpent for her sin.

What are some things we use to try to hide from God and cover our own sin? What excuses do we make for sin?

Adam not only failed to obey God, he failed to protect his wife. Theologians distinguish between sins of commission and sins of omission. As Darrin said it, we can fail by being "intentionally aggressive" or "intentionally passive."

What's an example of a sin of omission?

In which of your relationships or responsibilities are you prone to passivity? How can you be more vigilant and proactive?

The consequences of Adam and Eve's sin were real and lasting. But the good news is that their story didn't end behind trees and fig leaves. Even though they hid from God, He came to them. He even provided for them.

Read aloud Genesis 3:9 and 21.

Describe a way God has pursued you in a place or season when you weren't looking for Him.

What evidence of God's provision do you see? How is this provision evidence of His grace and love toward you?

What else has been challenging, encouraging, or insightful from today's study of Adam?

Conclude your group time with the prayer activity on the following page.

Pray

We all carry on Adam's legacy of passivity. Satan, our tempter and accuser, wants it that way. He wants us to give into temptation, seeking to be extraordinary on our own, turning away from God and other people. His primary weapons are lies to make us doubt God's goodness.

Spend a few minutes as a group naming lies that Satan speaks to us. Share a lie that is constantly whispered in your ear by the Enemy.

Read aloud the following passage from Peter's first letter. Close by praying for vigilance against the deadly lies of our Enemy and humble faith in God's goodness.

[6] Humble yourselves, therefore, under the mighty hand of God so that at the proper time he may exalt you, [7] casting all your anxieties on him, because he cares for you. [8] Be sober-minded; be watchful. Your adversary the devil prowls around like a roaring lion, seeking someone to devour.
1 Peter 5:6-8

Prayer Requests

Encourage people to complete This Week's Plan before the next group session.

This Week's Plan

In addition to studying God's Word, work with your group leader to create a plan for personal study, worship, and application between now and the next session. Select from the following optional activities to match your personal preferences and available time.

Worship

[ ] Read your Bible. Complete the reading plan on page 20.
[ ] Spend time with God by engaging the devotional experience on page 21.
[ ] Connect with God each day through prayer.

Personal Study

[ ] Read and interact with "The Process of Temptation" on page 22.
[ ] Read and interact with "Overcoming Temptation" on page 26.

Application

[ ] Identify some area of your life (home, work, school, neighborhood) where there is "chaos." Consider how you might bring order to that situation.
[ ] Memorize 1 Corinthians 10:13: "No temptation has overtaken you that is not common to man. God is faithful, and he will not let you be tempted beyond your ability, but with the temptation he will also provide the way of escape, that you may be able to endure it."
[ ] Seek out another believer (this person doesn't have to be in the group) with whom you might consider meeting on a semi-regular basis to ask each other questions about the temptations you face and to pray for one another.
[ ] Start a journal to record the times God has pursued you even when you've hidden from Him due to sin. Use this as a way to remind yourself of God's love and forgiveness when you feel the shame of sin.
[ ] Other:

Did you miss the group session?
Video sessions are available for purchase at *lifeway.com/extraordinary*

19

Read

Read the following Scripture passages this week. Use the acronym *HEAR* and the space provided to record your thoughts or action steps.

Day 1: Genesis 1

Day 2: Genesis 2

Day 3: Genesis 3:1-13

Day 4: Genesis 3:14-24

Day 5: Romans 5:12-21

Day 6: Romans 6:1-14

Day 7: 1 Corinthians 15:12-28

Reflect

TREE OF THE KNOWLEDGE OF GOOD AND EVIL

It's common for us to envision Adam and Eve walking around this lush garden, gazing upon the one beautiful fruit tree they have been told they can't "enjoy" right in the middle of it all. With this picture in mind, it's easy to wonder: *Did God set Adam and Eve up to fail?* We know Satan tempted them, but did God make it easier?

Let's look closer at how the Bible describes Eden, specifically the trees:

> Out of the ground the LORD God made to spring up every
> tree that is pleasant to the sight and good for food.
> **Genesis 2:9**

> When the woman saw that the tree was good for food, and that
> it was a delight to the eyes … she took of its fruit and ate.
> **Genesis 3:6**

Notice there are more than just a few trees in the garden. Also, notice the description of the tree of the knowledge of good and evil is essentially the same as all the other trees in the garden which they could enjoy. It wasn't any more pleasing or fruitful!

The way Satan tempted Adam and Eve was to have them forget about all the other trees. He wanted them to believe that God was withholding something good from them, that God was being stingy. The way we fight against temptation is by paying attention to all the other "trees" God has provided.

Identify ways God has blessed you with "pleasant" things to enjoy. Reflect on God's goodness by thanking Him for these gifts.

Personal Study 1

THE PROCESS OF TEMPTATION

The Book of James in the New Testament provides us with one of the clearest descriptions of how temptation works. In addition to discussing the Devil, our most obvious enemy, James identifies two other enemies we all have.

> [1] What causes quarrels and what causes fights among you? Is it not this, that your passions are at war within you? [2] You desire and do not have, so you murder. You covet and cannot obtain, so you fight and quarrel. You do not have, because you do not ask. [3] You ask and do not receive, because you ask wrongly, to spend it on your passions. [4] You adulterous people! Do you not know that friendship with the world is enmity with God? Therefore whoever wishes to be a friend of the world makes himself an enemy of God. [5] Or do you suppose it is to no purpose that the Scripture says, "He yearns jealously over the spirit that he has made to dwell in us"? [6] But he gives more grace. Therefore it says, "God opposes the proud, but gives grace to the humble." [7] Submit yourselves therefore to God. Resist the devil, and he will flee from you. [8] Draw near to God, and he will draw near to you. Cleanse your hands, you sinners, and purify your hearts, you double-minded.
> **James 4:1-8**

Our three enemies are the flesh, the world, and the devil.

1. The flesh is that part of us not yet submitted to God.

2. The world is the corporate expression of the flesh—many people living as if God does not exist.

3. The devil is a fallen angel who opposes God and His people.

How does each one of our enemies play upon our passions?

Of these three enemies, which one does James speak about most
in the passage you just read? What does the emphasis on that enemy
tell you about the nature of temptation?

A key to fighting temptation is to recognize that many sins are not merely
single acts but the result of an unchecked process. Look at how James
describes the process:

> [12] Blessed is the man who remains steadfast under trial, for when he has
> stood the test he will receive the crown of life, which God has promised
> to those who love him. [13] Let no one say when he is tempted, "I am
> being tempted by God," for God cannot be tempted with evil, and he
> himself tempts no one. [14] But each person is tempted when he is lured
> and enticed by his own desire. [15] Then desire when it has conceived
> gives birth to sin, and sin when it is fully grown brings forth death.
> **James 1:12-15**

James uses two metaphors to describe the process of temptation. The first (in v. 14) is a fishing metaphor. Even if you've never been fishing, you know the basic principle: you've got to hide the hook. You need bait. The reason sin looks good to us is because we are only seeing the bait. We are fish biting down on the hook. We focus on the short-term pleasure (the bait) and fail to see the long-term consequences (the hook).

Consider a current temptation you are experiencing.

What is the bait?

What is the hook?

The second (in v. 15) is a human growth metaphor—from conception to adulthood. All sinful actions begin as embryonic in the human heart—a tiny desire that begins to grow. Our whole beings are involved in this process. Our emotions latch onto something. *I want that. I have to have that.* Our mind rationalizes and justifies it. *It's not that bad. No one will see.* Then our will acts upon it. That tiny desire becomes an action that results in consequence. The seemingly harmless baby steps, a little thing here and there, lead us down a path into full-grown sinfulness that we never would've imagined. In the end, sin is always destructive.

So for each sin, we can ask the following questions: What is the embryo (desire)? What is the baby (action step)? What is the adult (consequence)?

Take lust for example. What is the embryo? *You are attracted to someone.* What is the baby? *You begin to fantasize about him or her.* What is the adult? *You have sex outside the marriage covenant.*

How would this growth process play out with anger?

Embryo:

Baby:

Adult:

Try it with another temptation. Identify the growth process from desire, to action, to consequence.

Embryo:

Baby:

Adult:

The wisdom that James provides us is crucial in understanding how temptation works. Even starting to identify this process in our own lives is an important tool for resisting temptation. In Personal Study 2, we'll look at how we can overcome temptation.

Close your study time in prayer, asking God for awareness of temptation and the strength to resist.

Personal Study 2

OVERCOMING TEMPTATION

Even though we have enemies from without (Satan and the world) and from within (the flesh), it's possible to resist temptation. Read these words from the apostle Paul:

> No temptation has overtaken you that is not common to man.
> God is faithful, and he will not let you be tempted beyond
> your ability, but with the temptation he will also provide the
> way of escape, that you may be able to endure it.
> **1 Corinthians 10:13**

How does Paul challenge you in this passage?

What hope does Paul give you in this passage?

One of the reasons we give into temptation is that we try to face it alone. We are prone to hide from God and one another—just like Adam and Eve.

Recall an occasion when you tried to overcome a recurring sin on your own. How much success did you have?

What fear(s) prevented you from confessing that struggle to someone?

Paul reminds us that we are not alone. Other people have experienced temptations like ours. Other people can identify with our struggle. So, we can turn to others for help. God Himself can identify with our struggle. Notice what the book of Hebrews says about Jesus and temptation.

> [17] Therefore he had to be made like his brothers in every respect, so that he might become a merciful and faithful high priest in the service of God, to make propitiation for the sins of the people. [18] For because he himself has suffered when tempted, he is able to help those who are being tempted.
>
> **Hebrews 2:17-18**

How does it make you feel to know that Jesus can relate to you in the temptations you face?

In your own life, what might it look like for Jesus to help you resist temptation?

Certainly one way, if not the most significant one, is through prayer—both His and ours. In what is often referred to as the High Priestly Prayer (see John 17), we see how Jesus prayed to the Father, specifically asking for protection—not just for His original disciples, but for all of His disciples: "I do not ask that you take them out of the world, but that you keep them from the evil one" (John 17:15). Now seated at the right hand of the Father, "he always lives to make intercession" for "those who draw near to God through him" (Heb. 7:25).

Jesus also receives our prayers. Believers are encouraged to "draw near to the throne of grace, that we may receive mercy and find grace to help in time of need" (Heb. 4:16). We come near "with confidence" (4:16) because Jesus is able "to sympathize with our weaknesses" since He "in every respect has been tempted as we are" (4:15). Jesus understands our struggle. His ears are open to us.

How does this image of Jesus as High Priest shape the way you pray?

The Gospels actually record Jesus' first encounter with Satan (see Matt. 4:1-11; Mark 1:12-13; Luke 4:1-13). After His baptism, Jesus was led into the wilderness to be tempted in preparation for His public ministry.

Read Matthew 4:1-11.

With what three things does Satan tempt Jesus?

How does Jesus respond each time?

How does Jesus' response shape the way you respond to temptation?

While we can look to Jesus as an example in our fight against temptation, we need more than someone to sympathize with us in our weakness. We need someone to save us from our sin. That is why it is of the highest importance that Jesus faced temptation "yet without sin" (Heb. 4:15). His sinless life was a necessary prerequisite to becoming the perfect sacrifice and through the cross, He not only resisted Satan but defeated him:

> ¹⁴ Since therefore the children share in flesh and blood, he himself likewise partook of the same things, that through death he might destroy the one who has the power of death, that is, the devil, ¹⁵ and deliver all those who through fear of death were subject to lifelong slavery.
> **Hebrews 2:14-15**

On the cross, Jesus "bruised" Satan's "head," whereas Satan only bruised "his heel" (Gen. 3:15). The first Adam was tempted by Satan and failed. Jesus, the "last Adam" (1 Cor. 15:45) was tempted by Satan and succeeded. Now we get to share in His victory.

Close your study time in prayer, thanking God for victory over sin and death.

Abraham

Week 2

Abraham was an old man when God called him to leave eveything behind for an even greater legacy.

Following God meant leaving his home and most of his family.

Following God meant leaving what was comfortable for what was unknown.

All Abraham had to rely on in making this decision was God's promise. He would bless Abraham, making him a great nation and a great name. This was an extraordinary promise for a man whose wife was barren.

But the blessing was not for Abraham alone. Through his offspring, God was going to bless "all the families of the earth" (Gen. 12:3).

Thousands of years later, we're now a part of that blessing and calling. God calls us to join in His redemptive mission. It brings Him greater glory to work *through* broken, sinful people than to work *around* them.

Responding to God's call means leaving something precious, but it's always in pursuit of the greater legacy God wants us to take part in.

Start

Welcome everyone back to the second group session.

Use the following content to start your time together.

At the end of group session 1, you were asked to look for areas where you are prone to passivity and vulnerable to the lies of the Enemy.

Is there an area of passivity in your life that you recognized for the first time? If so, would you be willing to share it with the group?

What did you learn about temptation as you completed your personal study of week 1?

How have you felt God's presence and pursuit of you this past week?

In week 1 we saw that God designed us for intimate relationship with Him and assigned us the great responsibility of stewarding His creation. But chaos entered the world through man's sin.

In the video for this session, Darrin explores the life of Abraham—one of the most well-known biblical figures, second only to Jesus. We'll see how God continues to pursue a relationship with His people by calling Abraham to leave a life of comfort and security for the sake of a greater mission and legacy.

Pray for God to open your hearts and minds before showing the video for session 2.

Watch

Use the space below to follow along and take notes as you watch video session 2.

If you want to understand a man, look at his _____,
his _____, and his _____.

Responding to God's call means _____ something precious.

A change in name means a change in _____ and a change
in _____.

God blesses us so we can be a _____.

Scriptures: Hebrews 11; Genesis 12-13,15,17,22

Discuss

Use the statements and questions below to discuss the video.

Despite the way history looks back on Abraham, Darrin explained that he started as an ordinary guy before God called him.

What are some ways you can relate to Abraham?

Darrin described three ways we avoid God's call:

1. Ignore—pretend God didn't say it

2. Question—act like we don't know what it means

3. Negotiate—argue with God about what He is asking us to do

When you sense God calling you to do something, which of these three avoidance responses comes most naturally for you?

Why do we sometimes try to avoid God's call in our lives?

Read aloud Genesis 12:1-9.

What does this passage reveal about God? About Abraham?

Darrin said that responding to God's call means leaving something precious.

What have been some of the more challenging things you've had to leave behind to follow God?

Darrin observed that in order to follow God, Abraham had to become a nomad—like the people to whom he likely felt superior most of his life.

How has God's call in your life exposed areas of pride in your heart?

Abraham also had to step into uncertainty. God was leading him to a new land but hadn't shown Abraham that land yet. Hebrews 11:8 echoes Genesis 12:1: "He went out, not knowing where he was going." Abraham had to act before he knew all the details.

> When was the last time following God meant walking into uncertainty for you?

> When you've sensed God calling you to act without knowing all the details, how have you found the faith to obey?

Read again God's call to Abraham in Genesis 12:1-3.

Ultimately what led Abraham to leave comfort and step into uncertainty was God's promise of a greater legacy. God's call was for Abraham, but it wasn't just about Abraham. There was a larger purpose. God blessed Abraham so that he would be a blessing.

> How have you seen believers use their positions of influence or material resources to bless the people and families in their communities?

> What are some tangible blessings God has given to you?

> What would it look like for you to be a blessing in your home? Your neighborhood? Your workplace?

> What else has been challenging, encouraging, or insightful from today's study of Abraham?

Conclude your group time with the prayer activity on the following page.

Pray

Individually, try to identify one thing (no matter how small it may seem) you sense God is calling you to leave to follow Him in a new way. Write your answers to the questions below in the space provided. After a few minutes, gather in smaller groups of two to three to share.

What is God calling me to leave?

What is uncertain about the result?

How might this serve to bless others?

Pray together that the answer to the third question would help you overcome any impulse to ignore, question, or negotiate with God.

Prayer Requests

Encourage people to complete This Week's Plan before the next group session.

This Week's Plan

In addition to studying God's Word, work with your group leader to create a plan for personal study, worship, and application between now and the next session. Select from the following optional activities to match your personal preferences and available time.

Worship

[ ] Read your Bible. Complete the reading plan on page 38.
[ ] Spend time with God by engaging the devotional experience on page 39.
[ ] Connect with God each day through prayer.

Personal Study

[ ] Read and interact with "Discovering God's Call" on page 40.
[ ] Read and interact with "Not Once, But Twice" on page 44.

Application

[ ] Memorize Genesis 12:2: "I will make of you a great nation, and I will bless you and make your name great, so that you will be a blessing."
[ ] Connect with someone from your group this week. Make an appointment to meet for coffee or lunch. When you meet, ask each other two questions: (1) Is there anything God is calling you to leave to follow Him? and (2) How can I help you in that? Then plan to follow up in the coming weeks.
[ ] To continue your journal, write down the different things you've had to leave behind to follow Jesus. Write down how God has provided.
[ ] Other:

Did you miss the group session?
Video sessions are available for purchase at *lifeway.com/extraordinary*

37

Read

Read the following Scripture passages this week. Use the space provided to record your thoughts and responses.

Day 1: Genesis 12:1-9

Day 2: Genesis 12:10-20

Day 3: Genesis 15:1-19

Day 4: Genesis 16:1-15

Day 5: Genesis 17:1-14

Day 6: Genesis 21:1-21

Day 7: Genesis 22

Reflect

WAITING PATIENTLY

Though Abraham is commended for his faith in the New Testament (see Heb. 11), his faith was by no means consistent. He was often impatient about his circumstances. Unwilling to wait for God, Abraham tried to take matters into his own hands and it backfired.

Not once, but twice, he lied and put his wife Sarah in danger because he didn't trust God's protection (see Gen. 12:10-20; 20:1-18). Even more devastating, Abraham doubted God's promise that Sarah would bear children and conceived a child through a female servant (see Gen. 16). His failure to trust God led to greater pain and dysfunction in his life and in the lives of others.

It's important to remember that our sin (even impatience when waiting on God's timing) doesn't only affect us. We saw this in week 1 with Adam, now with Abraham, and next week with Moses. It's a pattern of sin that's a struggle for each of us.

There are few commands in Scripture more difficult than waiting on God, but often they are connected to God's faithful provision. On his own Abraham would have utterly ruined himself and his family. But God was patient with Abraham.

God was faithful to deliver on his promises. We all find ourselves in times of waiting, hoping that our current circumstances will change. As you ask God for the patience to trust in His timing, reflect on this truth from Scripture:

> The LORD is good to those who wait for Him,
> to the soul who seeks him.
> Lamentations 3:25

Personal Study 1

DISCOVERING GOD'S CALL

Even if you've found Abraham relatable in certain ways after watching this week's video and participating in your group discussion, you may still be struggling with the nature of God's call. When God spoke to Abraham, it was so clear and direct. Why doesn't it feel that way for us?

In an important sense, Abraham's call was unique. He had a specific role within God's overall redemptive plan. But that doesn't mean we can't learn from Abraham's call. In fact, if we look more closely at what the Bible tells us about Abraham's call, we may find more encouragement there than we would at first glance.

For starters, notice that the Bible tells us Abraham received his call from God in two different locations. According to Genesis 11:31-32, God called Abraham in Haran. But when Stephen tells Abraham's story to the religious leaders of his day, he says that God called Abraham in Ur, "the land of the Chaldeans" before he lived in Haran (Acts 7:4).

So which one is it? While some skeptics may choose to believe that the New Testament or Stephen himself got it wrong, the answer is both. It is highly likely that God began to call Abraham while he was in Ur, and then when his father moved the family to Haran, God revealed even more to Abraham at that point. As we'll see next week, sometimes God grabs people's attention immediately, but often He does it incrementally.

How has discerning God's call in your life been incremental?

Not only can God's call vary in timing, it can vary in method. When we read about the apostle Paul's missionary journeys in the book of Acts, we know that the Holy Spirit guided him. Apart from direct revelation by the Holy Spirit, there were at least three different forms that guidance took.

1. God's clear priorities. The book of Acts opens with Jesus telling His disciples that they will be His witnesses in Jerusalem, Judea, Samaria and to the ends of the earth (see Acts 1:8). Similarly, the Gospel of Matthew ends with the Great Commission. Jesus commanded His disciples to go and make more disciples. The clear priority given to Paul was to preach the gospel to the Gentiles. He didn't always know where and how that would take place. But it oriented every decision he made.

What are some of the clear priorities that orient your decisions?

On a scale of 0-10 (0 = not at all and 10 = perfectly) how well do your priorities align with God's as revealed in Scripture?
Circle your answer.

0   1   2   3   4   5   6   7   8   9   10

What struggles impact the way you rated your priorities?

What would help you better align your priorities with God's?

2. God's response to prayer. While Paul was at the church in Antioch, the Holy Spirit said, " 'Set apart for me Barnabas and Saul for the work to which I have called them' " (Acts 13:2). But notice how that passage begins, "Now there were in the church at Antioch prophets and teachers," and "While they were worshiping the Lord and fasting, the Holy Spirit said ..." (13:1-2). It is clear that they were diligently seeking God's will before the Holy Spirit provided clarity.

> **What does prayer look like for you when you are trying to discern God's will?**

> **Who do you invite into that discernment process?**

3. God's response to our action. At times, our experience of this is more like trial and error. Consider how Luke describes one portion of Paul's journey, "They went through the region of Phrygia and Galatia, having been forbidden by the Holy Spirit to speak the word in Asia. And when they had come up to Mysia, they attempted to go into Bithynia, but the Spirit of Jesus did not allow them. So, passing by Mysia, they went down to Troas" (Acts 16:6-8). While it is entirely possible that the Holy Spirit directly spoke to Paul and Timothy in those places, they may have just experienced insurmountable obstacles that were understood as the Spirit closing doors. Either way, they went one way. Door closed. Then they went another direction. Door closed. After multiple unsuccessful attempts, the Holy Spirit finally told them where to go.

Discerning and following God's call will require risk as you take practical steps to align your priorities with His. Think back to the prayer activity that concluded your group discussion. Let's include today's steps of discernment.

What are you trying to discern about God's calling for your life?

How have prayer and/or closed doors provided clarity?

In what ways would stepping out in faith be costly?

What is risky or uncertain about it?

What risks are you currently taking that are aligned with God's priorities and undertaken in prayer?

How do you need to prioritize in order to take obedient action?

How could this step of faith bless others?

Pray that the answer to this last question would help you trust God in obedient action and risky faith for the sake of His mission.

Personal Study 2

NOT ONCE, BUT TWICE

In the "Faith Hall of Fame" in Hebrews 11, Abraham is commended not once, but twice, for leaving something precious in order to follow God. We've already discussed the first "leaving":

> [8] By faith Abraham obeyed when he was called to go out to a place that he was to receive as an inheritance. And he went out, not knowing where he was going. [9] By faith he went to live in the land of promise, as in a foreign land, living in tents with Isaac and Jacob, heirs with him of the same promise.
> **Hebrews 11:8-9**

Just to give us another picture of the significance of God's call to Abraham, Old Testament professor Sandra Richter translates it for our context:

> Leave your house, your job, your friends, your church, your relatives, abandon your inheritance, a 401K that will not transfer and maybe even the equity in your home—and go somewhere you don't speak the language, you have no business contacts, friends, or relatives ... and trust God to make a new place for you.[1]

But believe it or not, that may not have been as hard as the next "leaving" Abraham is commended for:

> [17] By faith Abraham, when he was tested, offered up Isaac, and he who had received the promises was in the act of offering up his only son, [18] of whom it was said, "Through Isaac shall your offspring be named."
> **Hebrews 11:17-18**

The first time Abraham encounters God is when he's asked to leave everything behind. There is no indication that he knew of God at all before that point. The only thing God could offer Abraham in his old age that he didn't already have was children. His wife Sarah was barren (see Gen. 11:30). God promising to "make of you a great nation" (12:2), implying offspring, was all Abraham needed to hear. Still it was no small thing for him to trust God to even provide in that way!

> Do you recall the first time you experienced God's call on your life (maybe through a parent, sibling, friend, youth group leader, or pastor)? Describe that experience. If you've never felt a specific calling, describe a time when you realized what God desired for you to do in general as a Christian.

> In all your questions and hesitations, was there one specific promise or hope that compelled you to follow Him?

> How long did you have to wait before you saw that promise fulfilled, that hope realized? Are you still waiting?

Already 75 years old, Abraham has to wait another 25 years before Isaac is born! Long before that point, he and his wife Sarah had lost not just patience but their trust that God would deliver on His promise. After listening to God's word for 10 years, Sarah says to Abram:

> "Behold now, the LORD has prevented me from bearing children. Go in to my servant; it may be that I shall obtain children by her." And Abram listened to the voice of Sarai.
> **Genesis 16:2**

It didn't help that Sarah immediately felt jealousy and anger toward Hagar when she conceived a son, Ishmael (despite it being her plan!). On top of that, he would not be the child of the promise. Despite the unbelief of Abraham and Sarah, and the dysfunction they introduced into their lives, God was gracious to Ishmael and blessed him, but He did not establish His covenant with him.

Displaying His extraordinary power within creation, God visited Sarah as he had promised, and she conceived and bore Isaac to Abraham when he was a hundred years old (see 21:1-7). After waiting a lifetime for their son, it must have felt like a blink of the eye before God sought to test Abraham. God told Abraham to sacrifice Isaac as a burnt offering (see 22:2).

What is your initial reaction to God's call here?

How do you make sense of this seemingly outrageous request?

Now consider how the Bible addresses Abraham's motivation for obedience:

> He considered that God was able even to raise him from the dead,
> from which, figuratively speaking, he did receive him back.
> **Hebrews 11:19**

Abraham was willing to "leave" Isaac because he knew God would be faithful to His covenant promises. Abraham knew that Isaac was his "only son" (11:17) with regard to the covenant. God's faithfulness was bound to Isaac's existence. Abraham knew that God would somehow resolve it. He had faith that God would remain faithful to His covenant even when it seemed there was no earthly way it would be possible.

Based on this discussion, how would you define faith?

Read Hebrews 11:1. How does this verse compare with your definition?

What does this verse add to your understanding of faith?

Pray now for faith that moves you to action, even when you can't see what God is doing and don't understand how it will all work out.

1. Sandra Richter, *The Epic of Eden* (Downers Grove, IL: Intervarsity Press, 2008), 158.

Moses

Any time God puts a call on your life, you're going to have questions.

You may have some doubts or even a few excuses as to why God should find someone else for the job. Some of this will be natural if God asks you to do things that make no earthly sense at all.

That was the case for Moses.

God called him to lead his people out slavery in Egypt. How was this fugitive shepherd with a speech problem supposed to stand up before Pharaoh and walk away alive—much less with all the Israelites following him?

And yet, God promised to be with Moses. When Moses finally overcame his reluctance, he found himself in the front row, watching God rescue His people and provide for them in spectacular and supernatural ways.

At some point along the way, however, Moses grew weary— as we all do when we try to fulfill God's call in our own strength. Leading a stubborn and stiff-necked people with short-term memory, Moses gets frustrated and makes the biggest mistake of his life trying to exercise his own will above God's—one that would prevent him from entering the promised land.

Start

Welcome everyone back to the third group session.

Use the following content to start your time together.

In the previous group session you were asked to consider something (no matter how small it may seem) that God is calling you to leave to follow Him.

> **As you spent time in God's Word and in prayer this week, did you sense God calling you (or reminding you of His call) to do something?**

> **Did you take any steps of faith in response to His call this week? If so, what did you do? If not, why not?**

> **From your personal study of week 2, what were some of your key takeaways on waiting, God's guidance, and faith?**

In this session we'll learn more about how God's call on our lives is for the sake of others. It's about us, but it's not about us. We'll explore the life of Moses, who wrestled with doubt even as he led the Israelites out of bondage in Egypt. Let's watch as Darrin connects Moses' story to our story.

Pray for God to open your hearts and minds before showing the video for session 3.

Watch

Use the space below to follow along and take notes as you watch video session 3.

God is _____, but He's also _____.

Anytime God puts a call on your life, you'll have _____.

Moses is tired, frustrated, and disconnected from God when he makes the biggest _____ of his life.

What happens to Moses is what happens to us. We try to accomplish _____ in our own strength.

God will work in _____ and through _____, despite _____.

Scriptures: Exodus 3:5-8; 11-12; Numbers 12:3-8; 20:2-13; Isaiah 6:1-5; Proverbs 14:4

Discuss

Use the statements and questions below to discuss the video.

Darrin picked up Moses' story from when God called him in the wilderness. But let's be reminded of why Moses was in the wilderness in the first place.

Read aloud Exodus 2:11-15.

As we see from this passage, Moses tried to do something about the pain he saw, but his violent response only added to the pain. So he hid in the wilderness as a fugitive and tried to start over with a new family.

> **When have you tried to fix a broken situation but ended up only adding to the brokenness?**
>
> **How does that past experience currently play into how you engage broken situations?**
>
> **What does God's appearance in the wilderness reveal about God?**
>
> **Why do you think God chose to meet Moses in the wilderness?**
>
> Darrin said that God's attention-getting devices are invitations for us to ponder and behold His character. Specifically, through the burning bush, God was revealing Himself as both holy and compassionate.
>
> **What are some things God has used to get your attention?**

Even though God revealed Himself in such a dramatic way, Moses questioned whether he could really do what God was calling him to do.

Read aloud Exodus 4:1-14.

> **Why do you think Moses doubted despite the signs God gave him?**

Despite Moses' objections and reluctance, God still does extraordinary things through him. Here are a just a few: parting the Red Sea (see Ex. 14), bringing water out of the rock (see Ex. 17), delivering the Ten Commandments (see Ex. 20). And through it all, God was with Moses. Consider how Exodus 33:11 describes the closeness of their relationship, "The LORD used to speak to Moses face to face, as a man speaks to his friend."

How does it make you feel to know that God blessed someone who was doubtful with such a close relationship?

Moses was constantly frustrated by the grumbling and complaining of the people. Instead of resting in his relationship with God, he again tried to accomplish God's work in his own strength. As Darrin explained from Numbers 20, Moses vented his frustration in a sinful way, cursing the people and disobeying God's clear command.

How do you know when you are trying to do God's work in your own strength?

What do you think is at the root of your attempts to act out of your own strength?

When are you most prone to frustration and doubt?

What do you think it looks like to invite God into your frustration?

Where in Moses' story can you find confidence that God will treat you with compassion?

What else has been challenging, encouraging, or insightful from today's study of Moses?

Conclude your group time with the prayer activity on the following page.

Pray

Despite having such unique access to God, Moses often locked his eyes on his own limitations and his frustration with other people. Isn't that the case for all of us? This caused him to lose sight of promises from God like this one:

> My presence will go with you, and I will give you rest.
> **Exodus 33:14**

We are prone to a similar struggle in the task before us as followers of Christ. Let's read aloud "The Great Commission" at the end of Matthew's gospel:

> [16] Now the eleven disciples went to Galilee, to the mountain to which Jesus had directed them. [17] And when they saw him they worshiped him, but some doubted. [18] And Jesus came and said to them, "All authority in heaven and on earth has been given to me. [19] Go therefore and make disciples of all nations, baptizing them in the name of the Father and of the Son and of the Holy Spirit, [20] teaching them to observe all that I have commanded you. And behold, I am with you always, to the end of the age."
> **Matthew 28:16-20**

Write these two passages on opposite sides of an index card or piece of paper to keep with you this week. Any time you feel doubtful or frustrated, look at these verses to remind yourself of God's promise of His power and presence to fulfill His calling.

Pray now for confidence in our extraordinary God who is always with us.

Prayer Requests

Encourage people to complete This Week's Plan before the next group session.

This Week's Plan

In addition to studying God's Word, work with your group leader to create a plan for personal study, worship, and application between now and the next session. Select from the following optional activities to match your personal preferences and available time.

Worship

[ ] Read your Bible. Complete the reading plan on page 56.
[ ] Spend time with God by engaging the devotional experience on page 57.
[ ] Connect with God each day through prayer.

Personal Study

[ ] Read and interact with "The Pitfalls of Leadership" on page 58.
[ ] Read and interact with "Tearing Down Our Idols" on page 62.

Application

[ ] Memorize Exodus 19:4-6: "You yourselves have seen what I did to the Egyptians, and how I bore you on eagles' wings and brought you to myself. Now therefore, if you will indeed obey my voice and keep my covenant, you shall be my treasured possession among all peoples, for all the earth is mine; and you shall be to me a kingdom of priests and a holy nation."
[ ] Update your journal by writing down the self-doubts that are preventing you from taking more of a leadership role in your home, your workplace, your church, or your community. For each doubt you list, write down how God would respond to you like He did to Moses in Exodus 3.
[ ] Connect with a close friend this week either in person or over the phone. Share with him or her some of the things you've learned so far in this study or even some of the things you've written in your journal.
[ ] Other:

Did you miss the group session?
Video sessions are available for purchase at *lifeway.com/extraordinary*

55

Read

Read the following Scripture passages this week. Use the space provided to record your thoughts and responses.

Day 1: Exodus 2

Day 2: Exodus 3

Day 3: Exodus 4

Day 4: Exodus 16

Day 5: Exodus 17

Day 6: Numbers 14

Day 7: Numbers 20:1-13

Reflect

GOD-HONORING RELUCTANCE

Moses was reluctant when God first called him to lead the people of Israel out of Egypt. His reluctance was dishonoring to God because it was focused more on his limitations than his Creator.

Read Exodus 4:10-11.

You'd think after seeing God perform so many signs and wonders in delivering the people of Israel out of Egypt that Moses would've transformed into the most confident leader imaginable. But when God called him to lead the people into the promised land, Moses was reluctant once again.

His initial reluctance was driven by doubt, but this time it was an expression of humility and dependence upon God.

> If your presence will not go with me, do not bring us up from here.
> **Exodus 33:15**

Moses took his eyes off himself, and asked God to show him His "glory" (33:18). Whereas God had expressed His anger to Moses at his initial reluctance (see 4:14), God revealed His "goodness" to him in a mysterious but tangible way (33:19-23).

When facing a decision to take action, consider whether any hesitation is coming from doubt or dependence.

Ask God to show you His goodness so that you might overcome any doubt-driven reluctance and desire nothing more than His presence and glory.

Personal Study 1

THE PITFALLS OF LEADERSHIP

At his lowest point as a leader (see Num. 20:2-13), Moses disobeys God and curses the people. At Meribah, where God had previously provided water for the people, Moses strikes the rock with his staff when God commanded him to speak to it. As a result, Moses was not permitted to enter into the promised land.

Numbers 20 does not record for us a random, isolated incident, but rather the culminating expression of rage due to issues within Moses' heart left unresolved for too long. It was the eventual end result of a downward spiral through frustration, fatigue, loneliness, and bitterness—pitfalls common for all leaders.

Frustration

Frustration was a constant reality for Moses in his leadership. His frustration was a result of his own insecurity and the ongoing resistance of the people to God's plan. Over and over again, the people would complain to Moses about the lack of food and water. Often the people expressed their opposition by idealizing their life in Egypt.

> Would that we had died by the hand of the LORD in the land of Egypt, when we sat by the meat pots and ate bread to the full, for you have brought us out into this wilderness to kill this whole assembly with hunger.
> **Exodus 16:3**

Over and over again the people "grumbled against Moses" and complained about their circumstances (Ex. 15:24; 16:2; 17:3; Num. 11:1; 14:2). Few leaders in the Bible experienced such constant resistance like Moses did (which is why none of that generation made it into the promised land).

Imagine what it would have been like in Moses' situation. How would you have responded to all the grumbling and complaining?

When have you experienced constant resistance toward you in a position of leadership or authority? How did you respond?

Fatigue

When Jethro, Moses' father-in-law, visited Moses in the wilderness and saw him handling all the people's disputes from morning till evening, he responded:

> ¹⁷ What you are doing is not good. ¹⁸ You and the people with you will certainly wear yourselves out, for the thing is too heavy for you. You are not able to do it alone.
> **Exodus 18:17-18**

Jethro knew that Moses was going to burn out if he didn't start delegating responsibility to other leaders. Moses listened to his father-in-law's advice and appointed others to deal with the small matters while he judged the great ones. Moses began sharing "the burden" (18:22) of leadership with others.

What is causing fatigue in your life?

What "burdens" do you need to share with others?

Loneliness

Exodus records only one instance of Moses experiencing true fellowship with God and a team of leaders after implementing Jethro's advice.

> [9] Then Moses and Aaron, Nadab, and Abihu, and seventy of the elders of Israel went up, [10] and they saw the God of Israel. There was under his feet as it were a pavement of sapphire stone, like the very heaven for clearness. [11] And he did not lay his hand on the chief men of the people of Israel; they beheld God, and ate and drank.
> **Exodus 24:9-11**

From there Moses ascended the mountain to receive the tablets of stone on which the law and commandments were written (see 24:12). But while Moses was on the mountain for 40 days and 40 nights (see 24:18), the people grew restless and called upon Aaron, "Up, make us gods who shall go before us. As for this Moses, the man who brought us up out of the land of Egypt, we do not know what has become of him" (32:1). Aaron listened and directed the people in creating the golden calf.

The same leaders with whom Moses had shared a meal in the presence of God to confirm the covenant, abandoned him. Aaron gave into the people's idolatry, and the elders (not mentioned in chapter 32) did nothing to stop it. In Numbers 11:16-17, curiously similar to Exodus 18, God directs Moses to appoint 70 men to serve as elders and officers of the people. We are never told what happened to the first 70 elders, but it's safe to assume they were disqualified from leadership after the golden calf incident.

How have you experienced loneliness?

When have you felt abandoned by a friend or fellow leader?

Bitterness

Hard-pressed by frustration, fatigue, and loneliness, Moses grows bitter. In Numbers 11, Moses begins expressing that bitterness. Not surprising, the complaints of the people are the occasion.

> [11] Moses said to the LORD, "Why have you dealt ill with your servant? And why have I not found favor in your sight, that you lay the burden of all this people on me? [12] Did I conceive all this people? Did I give them birth, that you should say to me, 'Carry them in your bosom, as a nurse carries a nursing child,' to the land that you swore to give their fathers? [13] Where am I to get meat to give all this people? For they weep before me and say, 'Give us meat, that we may eat.' [14] I am not able to carry all this people alone; the burden is too heavy for me. [15] If you will treat me like this, kill me at once, if I find favor in your sight, that I may not see my wretchedness."
> **Numbers 11:11-15**

In his bitterness, Moses does not see the situation accurately. He internalizes the people's rejection, failing to see that it is God they reject. "The anger of the LORD blazed hotly, and Moses was displeased" (11:10) but for different reasons. As Old Testament scholar Timothy R. Ashley writes:

> Moses does not react against the people's rejection of God's provision but against the people for making his job as a leader more difficult, and against Yahweh for giving him the task as a leader.[1]

In his bitterness, Moses can only see his frustration, fatigue, and loneliness. He loses sight of all the extraordinary ways in which God has provided in the past. He cries out, "Where am I to get meat to give to all this people?" (11:13), having completely forgotten that God had already miraculously provided for them in the past (see Ex. 16)!

In what ways has God provided for you in the past that you are forgetting in your own bitterness and anger? Remind yourself of these provisions and blessings when you're tempted to forget His goodness.

Personal Study 2

TEARING DOWN OUR IDOLS

In *Counterfeit Gods*, Tim Keller writes, "To contemporary people the word *idolatry* conjures up pictures of primitive people bowing down before statues."[2] Given our cultural distance from the Old Testament, we can read how the Israelites worshiped the golden calf (see Ex. 32) and come away with the impression that idolatry isn't a problem for our enlightened, contemporary society.

But the concept of idolatry is so much more than giant golden calves and little figurines. In Romans I, Paul gives a brief explanation of idolatry:

> [21] For although they knew God, they did not honor him as God or give thanks in him, but they became futile in their thinking, and their foolish hearts were darkened. [22] Claiming to be wise, they became fools, [23] and exchanged the glory of the immortal God for images resembling mortal man and birds and animals and creeping things.
> **Romans 1:21-23**

According to Paul, idolatry is taking anything within creation as our object of worship instead of our Creator. We can make an idol out of anything.

There are a number of ways to identify idols in our lives, but Tim Keller provides one definition that is particularly suited for understanding the root idolatry in both the people of Israel and in Moses during their wilderness wanderings. "A counterfeit god is anything so central and essential to your life that, should you lose it, your life would feel hardly worth living."[3]

Based on Keller's definition, what do you idolize?

The Israelites' Idol

It may be difficult at first to recognize the root idolatry of the Israelites given the oddity of the golden calf, but if we revisit many of the complaints they made toward God and Moses, it becomes a bit clearer that comfort was their primary idol. This idol says, "Life only has meaning/I only have worth if I have this kind of pleasure experience, a particular quality of life."[4] The Israelites often expressed this through their longings for food:

> [4] Now the rabble that was among them had a strong craving. And the people of Israel also wept again and said, "Oh that we had meat to eat!
> [5] We remember the fish we ate in Egypt that cost nothing, the cucumbers, the melons, the leeks, the onions, and the garlic. [6] But now our strength is dried up, and there is nothing at all but this manna to look at."
> **Numbers 11:4-6**

Time and time again, in complaining about their current situation, the Israelites would idealize Egypt. The people describe the fish as costing nothing and talk about their strength being dried up. In reality, the fish cost everything, as they were slaves in Egypt who were constantly worked to exhaustion.

The idol of comfort distorted their thinking to the point that they preferred bondage in Egypt above freedom in the promised land. The idol of comfort also prevented them from remembering the many extraordinary ways God provided for them—including food and drink.

What "cravings" keep you from enjoying what God has already given you?

While Israel, God's "son" (Ex. 4:22) complained about the food given to them, Jesus, the son of God, told His disciples, "'My food is to do the will of him who sent me and to accomplish his work'" (John 4:34). Accomplishing the will of the Father meant great sacrifice on His part, and yet Jesus found satisfaction in fulfilling His mission.

How is the love of comfort preventing you from participating in God's redemptive mission?

As believers, we can find strength to overcome the idolatry of comfort by remembering that Jesus is "the bread of life" (John 6:48). Israel "ate the manna in the wilderness and died," but Jesus provides "the bread that comes down from heaven, so that one may eat of it and not die" (6:49-50). Through the power of the Holy Spirit, we can partake of "the living bread" (6:51), which reminds us that this life is not all there is.

Moses' Idols

In Personal Study I, we looked at a number of pitfalls that contributed to the infamous Numbers 20 incident. While Moses was faithful to God in a way that the people never were, his disobedience in that moment cost him the opportunity to enter the promised land. There was an underlying idolatry in his own heart, as there is for each of us.

It is hard to identify the primary idol within Moses' heart, but it seems approval was an issue for Moses. The idol of approval says, "Life only has meaning/I only have worth if I am loved and respected by this person."[5]

For those who struggle with approval, their greatest nightmare is rejection. It would seem that Moses was living his nightmare. As we looked at Numbers II in the previous session, we observed that Moses internalized the people's rejection of God's provision. How many times had the people complained against him? Enough to provoke Moses to ask that God take him out of his misery immediately (see Num. II:15).

It's also possible that Moses dealt with the idol of power, which says, "Life only has meaning/I only have worth if I have power and influence over others."[6] Any leader would have had difficulty leading the Israelites in those circumstances, but it seems that Moses was especially enraged by the hard-heartedness of the people. He certainly must have felt powerless dealing with constant complaints and rebellion. When he struck the rock and cursed the people at Meribah, he was trying to exert his own power and judgment apart from God.

How might approval and power be idols for you?

How do you typically handle rejection?

Where in life do you feel powerless? How do you typically respond in those situations?

It is hard to know what caused these idols to have sway over Moses' heart, but in part we know that Moses questioned God's call for him from the very beginning. Even after seeing God perform several extraordinary signs, he still begged God to have someone join him before Pharaoh.

We can fight against approval and power by embracing the gospel truth that we are loved despite our performance because of Jesus' death in our place. We also see the gospel played out in the life of Jesus, the "prophet like Moses" (Acts 3:13-26; Deut. 18:15,18), who before ever preaching a sermon or performing a miracle received the Father's word of approval: " 'This is my beloved Son, with whom I am well pleased' " (Matt. 3:17). As we embrace those words for ourselves through the gospel, we will find strength to turn from our approval and power idols.

1. Timothy R. Ashley, *The Book of Numbers* (Grand Rapids: Wm. B. Eerdmans Publishing, 1993). 210.
2. Timothy Keller, *Counterfeit Gods: The Empty Promises of Money, Sex, and Power, and the Only Hope that Matters* (New York, Penguin Books, 2009), xi.
3. Keller, xviii.
4. Darrin Patrick, *Church Planter: The Man, the Message, the Mission* (Wheaton, IL: Crossway Books, 2010), 164.
5. Patrick, 164.
6. Patrick, 165.

Joshua

Week 4

Joshua, who spent many years as Moses' assistant, was God's choice to lead the people into the promised land. The majority of passages that deal with Joshua reveal to us some important truths about leadership.

One of the primary lessons we learn from Joshua's life is that good leaders are willing to take risks.

In fact, risk is at the heart of Christianity.

Taking God at His word, Joshua was willing to trust that God would work for his people in extraordinary ways. Joshua was willing to stick his own neck out because he understood God's call.

But being a risk-taker didn't mean fear was absent from Joshua's heart. That's why God was constantly reminding him to be strong and courageous. Joshua needed to grow in these areas. He learned to be courageous as he drew close to God in prayer—in both victory and defeat. As he reminded himself of God's promises over and over again, he gained strength.

Above all else, when we study Joshua's life, we discover that he was an exceptional leader because he was first and foremost a passionate worshiper.

Start

Welcome everyone back to the fourth group session.

Use the following content to start your time together.

We're halfway through *Extraordinary: Extraordinary God, Ordinary People.* Last week we looked at how God worked through Moses despite his doubts. We also attempted to see deeper into Moses' frustration and failure.

> As you completed your personal study of week 3, what did you learn about overcoming insecurity and dealing with what's going on beneath the surface?

> What was it like to carry with you God's promise from Exodus 33:14, "My presence will go with you, and I will give you rest"?

Over these last few weeks we've traced this process of "leaving" our comfort and doubts behind in order to lead. This week we're going to look at how God defines leadership and what it takes to join in His redemptive mission. Let's listen to Darrin on the leadership of Joshua, Moses' successor.

Pray for God to open your hearts and minds before showing the video for session 4.

Watch

Use the space below to follow along and take notes as you watch video session 4.

_____ is at the heart of Christianity.

Just because Joshua was a risk taker didn't mean he didn't have _____.

Fear is empowered by _____.

Community creates _____.

Step up and present yourself as a _____.

Scriptures: Numbers 13–14; Joshua 1–10; 24:15; Matthew 9:37-38; Hebrews 11:1

Discuss

Use the statements and questions below to discuss the video.

Let's begin where Darrin began by answering this question:

> **Have you ever been in a situation that needed a leader?**
>
> **In those situations do you tend to jump in right away or wait for someone else to take charge?**

Joshua stepped into a leadership position that had been held by Moses. Even though God did not permit Moses to lead the people into the promised land, he did extraordinary things as a leader.

> **When have you felt like you were in the shadow of someone else— someone who was well-known, well-liked, talented, or successful?**

One of the first things we find out about Joshua was that he and Caleb were the only spies who gave a good report about the land (see Num. 14:7). Joshua and Caleb saw the same land as the other 10 spies did. What distinguished them from the others was their willingness to trust God and look at the situation with the eyes of leaders. Let's read together how they responded to the people's desire to return to Egypt.

Read aloud Numbers 14:6-9.

> **What stands out to you about Joshua and Caleb's reaction?**

Let's consider how Darrin contrasted leaders and non-leaders:

1. Leaders step up when the situation looks bleak. Non-leaders bail.
2. Leaders are driven by opportunity. Non-leaders are driven by environment.
3. Leaders are led by the voice of God. Non-leaders are led by the voice of people.

Of these three descriptions, which one grabs your attention the most? Why?

Darrin said that "risk is at the heart of Christianity" and that "faith is always a risk."

What do those phrases mean to you?

How do they encourage or challenge you?

What are some examples of risks that you or people you know have taken as a result of following Jesus?

What is the relationship between risk and prayer?

In addition to being willing to take risks, Darrin said that good leaders learn to be courageous. This comes about through one's own devotion to God, but it is also learned through community.

When have you faced a risky step of faith and needed the support and encouragement of close friends and family?

How did your community of friends and family create courage to help you face a situation?

What else has been challenging, encouraging, or insightful for you from today's study of Joshua?

Conclude your group time with the prayer activity on the following page.

Pray

Darrin identified three lies that empower fear:

1. I can't be like _____.

2. God can't use me right now.

3. I can't influence people.

Which of these lies are you most prone to believe?

Each day between now and the next group session, pay attention to the times you sense yourself giving in to one of the three lies (or a similar one).

Use the occasions as opportunity to connect with God in prayer and to connect with a family member, friend, or someone in this group for encouragement.

As you share prayer requests and close in prayer, consider how God has ideally situated you to step up and lead in certain areas of your life.

Prayer Requests

Encourage people to complete This Week's Plan before the next group session.

This Week's Plan

In addition to studying God's Word, work with your group leader to create a plan for personal study, worship, and application between now and the next session. Select from the following optional activities to match your personal preferences and available time.

Worship

[ ] Read your Bible. Complete the reading plan on page 74.

[ ] Spend time with God by engaging the devotional experience on page 75.

[ ] Connect with God each day through prayer.

Personal Study

[ ] Read and interact with "How Godly Leaders Are Developed" on page 76.

[ ] Read and interact with "How Godly Leaders Show Courage" on page 80.

Application

[ ] Seek out your supervisor, group leader, or pastor this week. Whether you are currently leading something or not, ask him or her what your next step in leadership might be.

[ ] Memorize Joshua 1:9: "'Have I not commanded you? Be strong and courageous. Do not be frightened, and do not be dismayed, for the LORD your God is with you wherever you go.'"

[ ] Do a prayer walk around your neighborhood or workplace (you don't have to pray out loud) asking God to open an opportunity for you to get to know a neighbor or coworker better and the courage to engage in spiritual conversation.

[ ] Continue your journal this week by reflecting on the elder qualifications in 1 Timothy 3:1-7. These are characteristics modeled by elders for the entire church that can provide for us some (though not all) markers of maturity.

[ ] Other:

Did you miss the group session?
Video sessions are available for purchase at *lifeway.com/extraordinary*

73

Read

Read through the following Scripture passages this week. Use the space provided to record your thoughts and responses.

Day 1: Exodus 17:8-15; 33:7-11

Day 2: Numbers 13

Day 3: Deuteronomy 34; Joshua 1:1-9

Day 4: Joshua 4

Day 5: Joshua 6

Day 6: Joshua 23

Day 7: Joshua 24

Reflect

THE COMMANDER OF THE LORD'S ARMY

Just after Joshua had led the people across the Jordan River into the promised land, before they engaged in any battles, he had an extraordinary encounter.

> 13 When Joshua was by Jericho, he lifted up his eyes and looked, and behold, a man was standing before him with his drawn sword in his hand. And Joshua went to him and said to him, "Are you for us, or for our adversaries?" 14 And he said, "No; but I am the commander of the army of the Lord. Now I have come." And Joshua fell on his face to the earth and worshiped and said to him, "What does my lord say to his servant?" 15 And the commander of the Lord's army said to Joshua, "Take off your sandals from your feet, for the place where you are standing is holy." And Joshua did so.
>
> **Joshua 5:13-15**

This mysterious man was none other than God Himself. Joshua responds in worship to this man, whose very presence makes the place they are standing holy. Many acknowledge this as a pre-incarnate appearance of Christ.

Though in this situation and through most of his leadership, Joshua was pursuing the clear will of God, it would not always be that way for the people of Israel. They regularly presumed upon their status as God's chosen people to justify a whole host of sins. They wrongly believed that the covenant meant God would endorse their plans. They failed to see that the covenant meant God was committed to their ultimate good—not simply the good they wanted for themselves. Joshua was used greatly by God because he was more than a leader. He was first and foremost a worshiper.

Take time to consider the goals you've been pursuing. Are you participating in spiritual "activity" so that God will bless those plans? Or are you worshiping God with open hands, allowing His will to be done in and through your life?

Personal Study 1

HOW GODLY LEADERS ARE DEVELOPED

The book of Joshua begins with his commissioning as the new leader of the people of Israel, and it traces his leadership from that point until his death. The book ends by giving Joshua the highest praise any leader could receive.

> Israel served the LORD all the days of Joshua, and all the days of the elders who outlived Joshua and had known all the work that the LORD did for Israel.
> **Joshua 24:31**

But well before Joshua was a successful leader, when he was still a young man, he served as Moses' "assistant" (Ex. 24:13). The Bible does not specifically call Moses a mentor to Joshua, but we can infer that from their close relationship. When we look back through the books of Exodus, Numbers, and Deuteronomy, we get a glimpse of Joshua's development as a leader under Moses' mentorship.

The Bible does not provide us with a clear, step-by-step guide to leadership development, but by looking at Moses and Joshua's relationship there are at least three observations we can make about what good mentors do.

Good mentors provide relationship.

In last week's Personal Study 1, we read about the meal that Moses had with the leaders of Israel (see Ex. 24:9-11). This wasn't just about food; it was about fellowship—with God and with each other.

Immediately after "they beheld God, and ate and drank," the Lord calls Moses. Notice who accompanies him. "So Moses rose with his assistant Joshua, and Moses went up into the mountain of God" (24:13). This verse seems to indicate that Joshua took part in that fellowship meal with the "chief men of the people of Israel" (24:11)—even though Joshua was not numbered as one of the elders. Moses brought Joshua into that experience. Moses gave Joshua unprecedented access.

If you've had a mentor of any kind, how was the relationship helpful? If not, what would you hope to gain from a mentor relationship?

Good mentors provide responsibility.

Some people struggle to develop into the leaders they could be because they're never put into challenging situations. They may be given some menial tasks to do, but nothing of great consequence. Moses, on the other hand, gave Joshua tremendous responsibility—even at a young age. The first time we come across Joshua in the Bible is in Exodus 17:9. This chapter records the first battle that Moses and the people of Israel experience after being delivered from Egypt.

> 8 Then Amalek came and fought with Israel at Rephidim. 9 So Moses said to Joshua, "Choose for us men, and go out and fight with Amalek. Tomorrow I will stand on the top of the hill with the staff of God in my hand." 10 So Joshua did as Moses told him, and fought with Amalek, while Moses, Aaron, and Hur went up to the top of the hill.
> **Exodus 17:8-10**

If you were Joshua, how would you have responded to this request?

By taking on this responsibility, Joshua gained experience that clearly— given the book of Joshua—prepared him for future leadership. By submitting to Moses' direction, Joshua got an up-close view of God fighting for them in an extraordinary and mysterious way (see Ex. 17:11-13).

When have you been given a big responsibility? What did you learn through that process?

Good mentors provide correction.

In Numbers 11, God tells Moses to appoint elders to share in the burden of leading the people. God blesses these men with His empowering Spirit. As a result, the men begin prophesying, whereas before Moses had been the only one to do so. Hearing about this, Joshua says, "'My lord Moses, stop them'" (Num. 11:28). Moses responds:

> Are you jealous for my sake? Would that all the LORD's people
> were prophets, that the LORD would put his Spirit on them!
> **Numbers 11:29**

Joshua may have thought he was looking out for his mentor, but his protest revealed a mixture of self-protection and jealousy. Though Moses had expressed his displeasure with God shortly before this (recall "The Pitfalls of Leadership" study from last week), here he responded with the attitude of a godly leader—to see more leaders developed who know God intimately and are used by Him. Moses corrected Joshua's concern to protect Moses' unique position and by extension Joshua's own.

When is it hard for you to embrace what God is doing in the lives of people around you? When are you tempted to be jealous?

What attitudes in your own heart need correction from God and others?

Now that we've consider three things (relationship, responsibility, and correction) that good mentors give to emerging leaders, we need to observe the most significant aspect of leadership development—and it's something that good mentees do.

Good mentees love God more than they love leading.

Despite Moses' failings as a leader, he had an extraordinary relationship with God. "The LORD used to speak to Moses face to face, as a man speaks to his friend" (Ex. 33:11). But notice the second half of the verse:

> When Moses turned again into the camp, his assistant Joshua the son of Nun, a young man, would not depart from the tent.
> **Exodus 33:11**

The "tent of meeting" (a precursor to the tabernacle and later the temple) was a place of worship. It was where the people went to meet with God—primarily mediated through Moses and the priests. Some suggest that Joshua stayed in the tent of meeting to guard it in Moses' absence, but it certainly would have meant more than that for him. Earlier, he had accompanied Moses up the mountain where God spoke with Moses (Exodus 24:13). Being near God was not a task, but a privilege.

How can you avoid making your mentor(s) a substitute for God?

What are you doing to experience God's presence on a regular basis?

No matter how godly the people are in your life, no relationship is more important than your personal relationship with the Lord. Your goal is not to become more like any man or woman, but rather more like Christ.

Take time to prayerfully consider who can help you grow as a Christian and as a leader. Also pray about a person or small group of people whom God has put in your life in order for you to be a mentor to them—helping them grow to maturity as followers of Christ.

Personal Study 2

HOW GODLY LEADERS SHOW COURAGE

Three times in the first eight verses of Joshua I, God exhorts Joshua to be "strong and courageous" as He confirms him as leader of the people of Israel. God ends His commissioning speech with a command of encouragement and a promise.

> Do not be frightened, and do not be dismayed, for the LORD your God is with you wherever you go.
>
> **Joshua 1:9**

Fear was a natural response to what Joshua was about to undertake—leading the people of Israel in conquest of the promised land of Canaan. But to alleviate Joshua's fear, God promised to be with him and reassured him.

> No man shall be able to stand before you all the days of your life. Just as I was with Moses, so I will be with you. I will not leave you or forsake you.
>
> **Joshua 1:5**

In addition to promising His presence, God gave Joshua specific instructions. Considering the amount of attention given to battles and inheritance in the Book of Joshua, this is probably not the kind of instruction you would expect:

> [6] Be strong and courageous, for you shall cause this people to inherit the land that I swore to their fathers to give them. [7] Only be strong and very courageous, being careful to do according to all the law that Moses my servant commanded you. Do not turn from it to the right hand or to the left, that you may have good success wherever you go. [8] This Book of the Law shall not depart from your mouth, but you shall meditate on it day and night, so that you may be careful to do according to all that is written in it. For then you will make your way prosperous, and then you will have good success.
>
> **Joshua 1:6-8**

How does God define strength and courage for Joshua?

The key to Joshua's success in leading was his obedience to the book of the Law. God tells Joshua to meditate on it "day and night," so that it would shape all his thoughts and actions. The book of the Law was God's covenant with Israel, specifically referring to the whole of Deuteronomy 5–6 (including the blessings and curses of chapters 27 and 28), which Moses wrote down and read before the people.

The discipline of meditation (which included reading, praying, memorizing, and reflecting on God's law) was not merely a private spiritual exercise, but a vitally important habit that affected not just the life of a leader, but all under his leadership.

When do you spend time meditating on God's Word? What would it look like for you to have a consistent devotional life?

How does regular time of personal devotion affect your interaction with others? How does its absence affect interactions with others?

"Meditation" can be a loaded word. Many think of Eastern mystical religions or some process of emptying the mind. But biblical meditation is about filling the mind, specifically with thoughts of who God is and what He has done so that we might gain the strength and courage needed to follow Him.

> **Can you recall a recent situation in which the Holy Spirit brought to mind a verse or passage of Scripture? How did it impact your response in that situation?**

Even with an accurate view of biblical meditation, it may be hard to understand how God's specific command for Joshua to meditate on "the Book of the Law" would translate into strength and courage. The idea of meditating on the Law may seem more drudgery than delight. It is common for us to have a negative view of the Law. Often, we transfer our understanding of the scribes and Pharisees in Jesus' day as self-righteous onto all of the Old Testament saints.

There is so much that can be said regarding the heart of God's Law—more than our space here permits—but there are two key elements of the book of the Law to observe.

First, the book of the Law does not actually begin with commands. It begins with an acknowledgment of God's saving work:

> I am the LORD your God, who brought you out of the land of Egypt, out of the house of slavery.
> **Deuteronomy 5:6**

Before the cross, the exodus was the defining act of salvation for God's people.

Why is it significant that this is the start of the Law?

Second, the book of Law was not only meant to shape Israel's relationship with God, but their witness to the rest of the world.

> ⁶ Keep them and do them, for that will be your wisdom and your understanding in the sight of all peoples, who, when they hear all these statutes, will say, 'Surely this great nation is a wise and understanding people.' ⁷ For what great nation is there that has a god so near to it as the LORD our God is to us, whenever we call upon him? ⁸ And what great nation is there, that has statutes and rules so righteous as all this law that I set before you today?
>
> **Deuteronomy 4:6-8**

How does this passage inform your understanding of God's Law?

Compare verses 7 and 8. What is the connection between God's presence and the giving of the Law?

When we keep these two passages in view, we notice that the book of Law both points back to God's rescue of His people from bondage (salvation) and points forward to call the people to be a light to all other nations (mission). Their obedience was motivated from salvation and for mission. The Law did not in itself have the ability to supply Joshua with strength and courage, but it pointed to the Lawgiver who was with him and for him.

Job

Week 5

There is nothing more certain in a world stained by sin and permeated with brokenness than suffering. We know this to be true, and yet it doesn't prevent us from experiencing doubt and confusion when we do suffer.

It doesn't help when the common responses to suffering are that life is random or that our suffering is deserved.

Job dealt with both these responses from his wife and "friends," eventually crying out to God for an explanation, "Why?"

Job never gets his question answered, but he does get God. Even without an answer, he encounters God in such a powerful way that he repents of his attempts at self-justification. As his world is crumbling, Job discovers that God's presence is enough.

Through Job's story, we get a glimpse of what it means to be a good counselor to those suffering and are confronted with the fact that everything we have is a gift from God. We didn't earn it and we can't control it. But as we hold all we have been given with open hands, we can see God more clearly than ever—even through our suffering.

Start

Welcome everyone back to the fifth group session.

Use the following content to start your time together.

Over the last two weeks, we've looked at two major leaders from the Old Testament: Moses, who led the people out of bondage in Egypt and Joshua, who led the people into the promised land. Through these men, we've considered some major themes regarding leadership: doubt, fear, trust, courage, and obedience.

> **What did you discover this past week about the character of a godly leader?**

> **What is one thing you've learned in your study so far that you are trying to apply in your home, workplace, school, or community?**

At some point in our lives we realize that things don't always go well. God's favor doesn't always look like blessing, influence, and success. So what do we do when things don't go right? Does it mean we're doing something wrong? Do bad things really happen to good people?

Given how much we've talked about God's promises and provisions over the last four weeks, we need to spend some time dealing with suffering—the primary focus in the Book of Job.

Pray for God to open your hearts and minds before showing the video for session 5.

Watch

Use the space below to follow along and take notes as you watch video session 5.

When people suffer they try to _____.

We all try to make a case for why we shouldn't be _____.

It's good to ask God _____ as long as you're OK with getting a _____ back.

Sometimes people don't need your _____, they just need _____.

Job never got an _____ or vindication, but he did get _____.

You know you're seeing _____ when you see everything in your life as _____.

Scriptures: Job1:1-5; 2:9; 4:7-8; 38:4; 2:13; 9:17; 38:1; 42:5-6; 1:21

Discuss

Use the statements and questions below to discuss the video.

Both inside and outside the church we find a variety of responses to suffering, but Darrin identified two primary ones:

1. The humanist says "life is random," therefore suffering is random.
2. The moralist says "life is cause and effect," therefore suffering is deserved.

> **When you see or experience suffering, what is your default response? If you go back and forth between the two, what explains the shift?**

Darrin compared the humanist response to Job's wife, "'Do you still hold fast your integrity? Curse God and die'" (Job 2:9). Then he compared the moralist response with Job's friends (Eliphaz, Bildad, and Zophar), "'Who that was innocent ever perished? Or where were the upright cut off?'" (Job 4:7).

Job described his wife (the humanist) as "foolish" (Job 2:10) and his friends (the moralists) as "worthless physicians" (13:4).

> **Why is the humanist response "foolish" and the moralist response "worthless"?**

Darrin explained that one of the fruits of personal suffering is that it can make us good counselors.

> **How can your suffering help you minister to someone else?**

> **How has someone else's empathy through similar suffering helped comfort you in your own experience? How has someone else ministered to you through their quiet presence?**

> **When has someone's advice or explanation been hurtful rather than helpful in a time of suffering or confusion?**

Have you ever sat quietly with someone suffering? How difficult was it to be silent? What challenges did you face while sitting quietly?

Darrin told us that there were two things Job wanted from God in his suffering—vindication and explanation. He wanted to hear that he did nothing wrong (and wanted his "friends" to hear that, too) and he wanted to know why this was happening to him. God responds to Job, but God never answers the why question.

What do you think drives us to ask why? What are we hoping to find out by asking?

How would knowing why help?

Darrin mentioned two other fruits of suffering: that we can see God more clearly and that we can be transformed by grace. Though Job did not receive the reply he was expecting, he did get something extraordinary.

Read aloud Job 38:1-11.

How would you summarize what God is doing through His response? How is this response "grace" to Job?

How does God's response encourage you in your own suffering?

Read Job's response to God in Job 42:5-6.

How did Job's view of God change? How does this change Job's response to his own suffering?

When have you experienced God in a different way while suffering?

What else has been challenging, encouraging, or insightful from today's study of Job?

Conclude your group time with the prayer activity on the following page.

Pray

In Job we see someone who suffered immensely and never found out why he was suffered, but he experienced God in an extraordinary way. Beholding God in this way did not remove Job's pain, but it did transform him.

Is anyone in your group currently in a painful situation? How can you quietly comfort him or her?

Read 1 Peter 5:6-11.

In our personal study this week, we're going to look at the primary way God speaks to us in our pain and suffering through the life and death of Jesus, the Son of God, who was there when the Father "laid the foundation of the earth" (Job 38:4).

As you share prayer requests and close in prayer, ask the Holy Spirit to fill you with a sense of the pain and suffering that Jesus endured so we can find comfort to endure our own pain and in turn comfort others who are suffering.

Prayer Requests

Encourage people to complete This Week's Plan before the next group session.

This Week's Plan

In addition to studying God's Word, work with your group leader to create a plan for personal study, worship, and application between now and the next session. Select from the following optional activities to match your personal preferences and available time.

Worship

[ ] Read your Bible. Complete the reading plan on page 92.
[ ] Spend time with God by engaging the devotional experience on page 93.
[ ] Connect with God each day through prayer.

Personal Study

[ ] Read and interact with "God's Purpose for Our Suffering" on page 94.
[ ] Read and interact with "God's Own Experience of Suffering" on page 98.

Application

[ ] Make a list of people you personally know who are enduring pain and loss right now. Spend time praying for them and, as the Spirit guides you, write a note or make a call letting them know you are praying for them.
[ ] Read through all of God's response to Job in chapters 38-41. Consider reading it out loud as a way to increase your concentration on the text.
[ ] Memorize Job 42:5-6: "'I had heard of you by the hearing of my ear, but now my eye sees you; therefore I despise myself, and repent in dust and ashes.'"
[ ] Continue writing in your journal by acknowledging some personal suffering that caused (and may still cause) you to question God's goodness. Ask God to help you make sense of that experience or find peace apart from explanation.
[ ] Other:

Did you miss the group session?
Video sessions are available for purchase at *lifeway.com/extraordinary*

91

Read

Read through the following Scripture passages this week. Use the space provided to record your thoughts and responses.

Day 1: Job 1

Day 2: Job 2

Day 3: Job 8–9

Day 4: Job 13

Day 5: Job 23

Day 6: Job 38

Day 7: Job 42

Reflect

POETIC LAMENT

The book of Job is narrative unlike what we've come across in Genesis–Joshua. It is best understood as wisdom literature, a genre of Scripture that includes Psalms, Proverbs, and Ecclesiastes. Some also find similarities within Song of Solomon, Ruth, and Lamentations. Many of these books are more poetic than prosaic in nature. We are not meant to merely search for the doctrine, but to consider the vast range of human emotion that is given voice.

Consider the fact that God has chosen to reveal Himself through a variety of literary genres. He cares not only about history and law, but also emotion and beauty. He desires to relate to us in every part of our being.

Job's speeches take the form of poetic lament. In form and style they resemble the laments found in the Psalms, which has been considered the prayer book or songbook of God's people. It is interesting that laments are one of the most frequent types of psalms. Old Testament scholar Tremper Longman, III describes the laments as "the psalmist's cry when in great distress he has nowhere to turn but God."[1]

Longman identifies three kinds of complaints found with the laments: (1) troubled over one's own thoughts and actions, (2) troubled over the actions of others against the psalmist, and (3) frustration with God Himself.[2] It is remarkable, if not shocking, to see such raw intensity and honesty within the book of Job and the lament psalms. God is not only OK with our honest emotions, Scripture reveals that they are part of a genuine relationship with God. See Psalm 10, 31, 39, 55, 77, and 142 for examples of lament.

Spend time prayerfully considering your own feelings, questions, or suffering. Voice your lament to God. Consider writing your own psalm of lament.

Personal Study 1

GOD'S PURPOSE FOR OUR SUFFERING

The Bible is full of tensions—two truths that seem contradictory on the surface but are in fact complementary. The tension regarding suffering is that it is both mysterious and meaningful.

In his book, *Walking with God through Pain and Suffering,* Tim Keller writes:

> Christianity teaches that, contra fatalism, suffering is overwhelming; contra Buddhism, suffering is real; contra karma, suffering is often unfair; but contra secularism, suffering is meaningful. There is a purpose to it, and if faced rightly, it can drive us like a nail deep into the love of God and into more stability and spiritual power than you can imagine.[3]

In our group time we discussed how suffering can help us see God more clearly. We considered how Job was changed by his encounter with God even though it was not what he expected:

> [2] I know that you can do all things,
>   and that no purpose of yours can be thwarted.
> [3] 'Who is this that hides counsel without knowledge?'
> Therefore I have uttered what I did not understand,
>   things too wonderful for me, which I did not know.
> [4] 'Hear, and I will speak;
>   I will question you, and you make it known to me.'
> [5] I had heard of you by the hearing of the ear,
>   but now my eye sees you;
> [6] therefore I despise myself,
>   and repent in dust and ashes.
> **Job 42:2-6**

Due to its poetic nature and its position within Scripture, the book of Job is more concerned with depicting rather than explaining the change that takes place through Job's suffering. We turn to the New Testament epistles, written in light of Jesus' incarnation, death, and resurrection, for more explanation on one purpose of suffering.

Read the following passages of Scripture and record how they contribute to your understanding of the purpose of suffering:

Romans 5:3-5

James 1:2-4

1 Peter 1:6-7

The 1 Peter passage provides us with the most vivid comparison for suffering. Our faith is compared to gold, a precious metal, that is exposed to extreme heat in order to remove its impurities. The fire is not intended to destroy, but refine the precious metal. Peter is saying, in the same way, trials are meant to shape our faith into its purest form.

How have you seen or personally experienced trials produce a greater, more pure faith?

What kinds of "impurities" do you think God is trying to remove from you through trials?

.

In these three passages, we are encouraged to "rejoice" in our sufferings. The point is not that we are meant to enjoy our pain, but to take joy in what the trial will produce in us. That is why our future hope is found within the surrounding context:

> Through him we have also obtained access by faith into this grace
> in which we stand, and we rejoice in hope of the glory of God.
> **Romans 5:2**

> Blessed is the man who remains steadfast under trial, for when he has
> stood the test he will receive the crown of life, which God has promised
> to those who love him.
> **James 1:12**

> [3] Blessed be the God and Father of our Lord Jesus Christ! According
> to his great mercy, he has caused us to be born again to a living hope
> through the resurrection of Jesus Christ from the dead, [4] to an inheritance
> that is imperishable, undefiled, and unfading, kept in heaven for you.
> **1 Peter 1:3-4**

How can being reminded of our future hope serve as a motivation for remaining steadfast through trials and suffering?

What would it look like for you to "embrace" the trials that God brings into your life?

Close your time of study by praying for God to help you embrace His transformative work in you through suffering. This doesn't mean trials are less painful or confusing. Trusting God in the midst of suffering means you are hopeful and believe that He will ultimately use the experience for good.

Personal Study 2

GOD'S OWN EXPERIENCE OF SUFFERING

As we saw in this week's reflection, various genres of literature are used to connect with people in different ways. Genre and language highlight different elements and nuances that reveal what the author—God through different people at different times in the case of Scripture—desires to communicate.

Word choice is just as important in contemporary culture as it was in ancient times. Language is rich in communicating not only facts but also values. Often different cultures will have multiple words to emphasize what may seem to others a subtle nuance. These distinctions help draw attention to something specific that's important to the communicator even if someone would otherwise understand the general meaning.

For example, it's interesting that the French language has two words for what we'd simply translate as "knowing."

One word is *savoir*, which refers to knowing about something or knowing how to do something.

The other word is *connaitre*, which refers to knowing someone.

This distinction, which is lacking in the English language, is useful as we consider what resources we have in Christianity for dealing with suffering.

In the previous study, while talking about the meaning and purpose of suffering, we focused more on the first type of knowing. It was about knowing the nature of the process. If we stop there, we may find the Christian response to be intellectually satisfying but not altogether comforting. The unique resource we have for dealing with suffering is Jesus Himself. God doesn't just know about pain, God has experienced pain. The pain of the cross is forever a part of the Trinity's memory.

The book of Job, just like the entire Old Testament, points toward Christ. While Job was a relatively innocent sufferer, Jesus is the only truly innocent sufferer. Apart for the passion narratives in the Gospels, few describe Jesus' suffering as vividly as the prophet Isaiah:

> ³ He was despised and rejected by men;
>   a man of sorrows, and acquainted with grief;
> and as one from whom men hide their faces
>   he was despised, and we esteemed him not.
> ⁴ Surely he has borne our griefs
>   and carried our sorrows;
> yet we esteemed him stricken,
>   smitten by God, and afflicted.
> ⁵ But he was pierced for our transgressions;
>   he was crushed for our iniquities;
> upon him was the chastisement that brought us peace,
>   and with his wounds we are healed.
> **Isaiah 53:3-5**

What emotions do you experience as you read this passage?

What difference does it make to you that we worship a God in Jesus Christ who was "a man of sorrows, and acquainted with grief" (v. 3)?

The very next line of this "Suffering Servant" passage displays another reason Jesus is the ultimate Job:

> He was oppressed, and he was afflicted,
> yet he opened not his mouth;
> like a lamb that is led to the slaughter,
> and like a sheep that before its shearers is silent,
> so he opened not his mouth.
> **Isaiah 53:7**

While Job sought to defend himself before God, Jesus willingly endured suffering so that we might have peace with God. Jesus knew why His suffering was necessary and what it would produce. In one sense this was crucial. Hebrews says it was "for the joy that was set before him" that Jesus "endured the cross" (12:2). But the meaningfulness did not remove the agonizing pain. The meaningfulness did not remove His need to wrestle with God the Father.

Read the Gospel accounts of Jesus in Gethsemane. How is the humanity of Jesus expressed in each one? What emotions and pains does Jesus experience as He approaches His death?

Matthew 26:36-46

Mark 14:32-42

Luke 22:39-46

Gethsemane would not be the last time Jesus prayed to God the Father before His death. On the cross, Jesus spoke the words:

> My God, my God, why have you forsaken me?
> **Matthew 27:46**

These are the opening words to Psalm 22. Read it if you have a few minutes. This psalm of David not only expressed feelings about his own circumstances, but prophetically points toward Jesus and His experience in crucifixion.

In His time of greatest agony, Jesus offered up the lament of an innocent sufferer. In our time of great need, we can offer up our own laments knowing that we have a God who can sympathize with us, having experienced it Himself.

> **If you didn't write out a psalm of lament during the reflection portion of this week's study, consider doing so now. If you did, feel free to write another one. Pour out your heart to God, knowing that He has suffered pain, and seek your hope in Jesus.**

1. Tremper Longman, III, *How to Read the Psalms* (Westmont, IL: Intervarsity Press, 2009), 26.
2. Ibid.
3. Tim Keller, *Walking with God through Pain and Suffering* (New York: Penguin Books, 2013), 30.

Esther

Week 6

The story of Esther shows us that God isn't just in the big and spectacular, but the small and ordinary as well. Not once is God ever explicitly mentioned, but there are evidences of His invisible hand throughout the book.

Esther isn't the picture of a perfect hero, but she is a timely one. The chain of events that led to her becoming queen was essentially beyond her control. The decisions she did make were often morally questionable but based on self-preservation.

When she realized that perhaps God had orchestrated it all for her to intervene on behalf of God's people, she changed. Realizing she had a role in what God was doing in the world, Esther put her life on the line.

Esther gives us confidence that God can use us to impact the lives of others through the positions of influence into which we've been placed and the needs around us.

More than that, Esther points to Jesus, who gave up the ultimate position, in the ultimate palace, and laid down His life so that we might be free from the enemies that try to destroy us.

Start

Welcome everyone back to the final group session.

Use the following content to start your time together.

We've arrived at our final week of *Extraordinary: Extraordinary God, Ordinary People.* Last week we explored the topic of suffering through the book of Job, which seemingly calls into question the goodness and character of God. And yet we considered how Job pointed us to Jesus, the only truly innocent sufferer.

> Are you beginning to see God in a new light? If so, how?

> Would you like to share a lament you wrote or what you gained from the experience of being honest with God about you feelings?

In the last five weeks we've studied the lives of people who experienced God in direct and amazing ways. But few of us encounter God in such miraculous fashion. So how do we respond when God seems distant?

In our final week of study, Darrin is going to walk us through the Book of Esther—a book of the Bible that surprisingly never mentions the name of God.

Pray for God to open your hearts and minds before showing the video for session 6.

Watch

Use the space below to follow along and take notes as you watch video session 6.

God uses Esther in her _____.

Pride causes us to constantly ask ourselves _____ questions.

A humble person is more interested in _____ you
than _____ by you.

God is at work _____.

Your talents and abilities were _____ to you so that God
can _____ you.

Scriptures: Esther; Esther 4:14; Matthew 4:19

Discuss

Use the statements and questions below to discuss the video.

Darrin recounted much of Esther's story. There was a lot in the video, so you'll read through the entire book (just 10 chapters) in your personal study.

How would you summarize the plot? What were the key points?

Esther is an unlikely hero. She's living in exile as an orphan who was taken against her will into a pagan king's harem.

On a scale of 0-10 (0 being *none* and 10 being *total*) how would you rate her influence over her situation at the beginning of the story? At the end of the story? Explain your ratings and any change.

Twice we read that Esther concealed her Jewish identity while in the harem at the command of Mordecai (see Esth. 2:10,20). It seems that she went along with every aspect of the "beauty pageant."

Do you think she did the right thing in her situation? Why or why not?

Without knowing the end of the story, what would you have done?

What does God's willingness to use Esther to save His people say about Him?

After Haman is promoted to the king' right hand, he has an encounter with Mordecai. Because Mordecai, revealing his Jewishness, will not bow down and pay homage, Haman is "filled with fury" (3:5). He plots to destroy all the Jews and successfully persuades the king to see them as a threat. Mordecai then appeals to Esther to use her position to save her people.

Read Esther 4:13-14.

If Mordecai believed that "relief and deliverance" would arise even if it didn't come through Esther, why did Esther risk her life?

Darrin used the question Mordecai posed to Esther as an entryway into discussing God's providence. The deliverance that God provides for His people is not obvious or spectacular, though it is still extraordinary.

How would you explain God's providence?

Looking back on your own life, how can you see God's hand bringing you to where you are today?

Darrin described Esther's appeal to the king as identification ("I am one of them.") and mediation ("Do not harm them.").

How is Esther's identification and mediation a picture of Jesus?

What would it look like for you to identify as one of God's people in your home, workplace, school, or neighborhood?

How might you be in a position to see people saved?

What are some "ordinary events" that you've seen God use to bring healing in your family, your workplace, or your community?

What else has been challenging, encouraging, or insightful from today's study of Esther?

As we conclude this study, what have you learned about God over the past 6 weeks? About your relationship with Him?

What has been the most practical takeaway helping you live out your faith in our extraordinary God?

Conclude your group time with the prayer activity on the following page.

Pray

We may never find our lives at stake, but we do risk our reputation and even some relationships when we identify ourselves as followers of Jesus. We can only take these risks when we trust that God is at work in and around our lives—even when we can't see how.

Spend some time now sharing ways God has been at work in your life since joining this small group.

As you close your time together, pray that God would help you see past all the things on the surface that could keep you from being used by Him. Ask the Holy Spirit to help you see the opportunities you have to be a blessing to others and a witness to the gospel of Jesus Christ.

Prayer Requests

Encourage people to complete This Week's Plan.
Discuss plans for what your group will study next now that you have completed
Extraordinary: Ordinary People. Extraordinary God.

This Week's Plan

In addition to studying God's Word, work with your group leader to create a plan for personal study, worship, and application between now and the next session. Select from the following optional activities to match your personal preferences and available time.

Worship

[ ] Read your Bible. Complete the reading plan on page 110.
[ ] Spend time with God by engaging the devotional experience on page 111.
[ ] Connect with God each day through prayer.

Personal Study

[ ] Read and interact with "Acknowledging Our Identity" on page 112.
[ ] Read and interact with "Providence and Responsibility" on page 116.

Application

[ ] Esther is the story of a woman who exercised the influence afforded her position for the good of a vulnerable group of people. Make a list of all the positions of influence you hold (no matter how small they seem). Pray that the Spirit would reveal to you how you can better leverage your influence for the sake of God's kingdom.

[ ] Memorize Esther 4:14: "'If you keep silent at this time, relief and deliverance will rise for the Jews from another place, but you and your father's house will perish. And who knows whether you have not come to the kingdom for such a time as this.'"

[ ] As you read through the book of Esther, write down all the "coincidences" you can find that point to God's providential care over Esther, Mordecai, and his people.

[ ] Other:

Did you miss the group session?
Video sessions are available for purchase at *lifeway.com/extraordinary*

109

Read

Read through the following Scripture passages this week. Use the space provided to record your thoughts and responses.

Day 1: Esther 1–2

Day 2: Esther 3

Day 3: Esther 4

Day 4: Esther 5

Day 5: Esther 6

Day 6: Esther 7–8

Day 7: Esther 9–10

Reflect

MY QUESTIONABLE PAST

Many of us live with the regret of past decisions. We expend so much energy avoiding or numbing our feelings of shame that we're unable to connect with God in the present. It often prevents us from taking risks because we doubt that God could—or even would—use us to make a difference in the lives of people around us.

Esther's story can give us confidence that God can not only use us to change the lives of others, but He can do that through our questionable past. Esther's story can also give us confidence that God works even through the parts of our past that we had no control over. The word that Mordecai has for Esther may be the one God has for you:

> Who knows whether you have not come to the kingdom for such a time as this?
> **Esther 4:14**

What opportunities has God put in front of you to advance His kingdom? Pray and ask the Spirit to reveal to you any shame and regret from your past. Meditate on the verses below as you consider how to step out in faith.

> There is therefore now no condemnation for those who are in Christ Jesus.
> **Romans 8:1**

> You did not receive the spirit of slavery to fall back into fear, but you have received the Spirit of adoption as sons, by whom we cry, "Abba! Father!"
> **Romans 8:15**

Personal Study 1

ACKNOWLEDGING OUR IDENTITY

As a result of their constant unfaithfulness to the covenant, God judged the nation of Israel by removing them from the land. The Babylonian exile was God's means of judgment. Life outside the land raised many questions for the Jews. Had God given up on His people entirely? How were they to remain faithful in a new society and culture whose values were often directly opposed to God? What did it mean to identify as one of God's people now?

The books of Esther and Daniel, exclusively concerned with the dealings of Jews during the Exile, raise those important questions. Esther's own growth in courage was directly connected to her willingness to identify as Jewish. Shortly into her story, we discover that she has been advised to conceal her Jewish identity by Mordecai. We don't know the exact reason, but perhaps it was out of fear that she would be treated even more horribly as a foreigner than what was already expected for a young girl within the king's harem. We do know that Esther had to reveal her identity to the king in order to intervene for God's people (see Esth. 7:4).

In what ways are you pressured to conceal your Christian identity?

What are some of the costs associated with revealing your Christian identity?

Even though many Jews eventually returned to Jerusalem, the land would continue to be occupied by one world superpower after the next. The entire New Testament was written within the context of the Roman Empire's virtual world-wide rule. Many of the questions asked by Jews during the exile continued to be the questions asked by the early church.

The apostle Peter uses the language of "exile" in his letter (1 Pet. 1:1,17) describing believers as "sojourners and exiles" (2:11). He did so to prepare the church for the persecution they would experience by claiming "Jesus is Lord," not "Caesar is Lord." Though the apostle Paul does not use the explicit language of exile, he does play on the concept of citizenship.

> [17] Brothers, join in imitating me, and keep your eyes on those who walk according to the example you have in us. [18] For many, of whom I have often told you and now tell you even with tears, walk as enemies of the cross of Christ. [19] Their end is destruction, their god is their belly, and they glory in their shame, with minds set on earthly things. [20] But our citizenship is in heaven and from it we await a Savior, the Lord Jesus Christ.
> **Philippians 3:17-20**

What does it mean that "our citizenship is in heaven"?

According to Paul, how is that spiritual reality practically expressed in our lives?

The language we come across in passages like these draw clear distinctions between those who follow Jesus and those who reject Him. And even though we are to seek "a better country, that is, a heavenly one" (Heb. 11:16), we are not called to dismiss the place where God currently has us.

Before He was betrayed and given up to die, Jesus interceded in prayer to the Father for His disciples:

> [14] I have given them your word, and the world has hated them because they are not of the world, just as I am not of the world. [15] I do not ask that you take them out of the world, but that you keep them from the evil one. [16] They are not of the world, just as I am not of the world. [17] Sanctify them in the truth; your word is truth. [18] As you sent me into the world, so I have sent them into the world. [19] And for their sake I consecrate myself, that they also may be sanctified in truth.
>
> [20] I do not ask for these only, but also for those who will believe in me through their word, [21] that they may all be one, just as you, Father, are in me, and I in you, that they also may be in us, so that the world may believe that you have sent me.
> **John 17:14-21**

As Christians we are called to be distinct from the world even as we are "sent" into the world. This is the tension we experience as missionaries.

In this prayer, what does Jesus reveal as our purpose in the world?

Jesus is clear that we will face trials. What role does the truth of God have in the lives of believers?

What does it look like practically to be in your world but not of it?

Though Esther was not a "missionary," she was sent by God into her position as queen (though she did not know for what purpose). Before Haman's plot was concocted, God had Esther in place. By risking her life and revealing her identity to the king, she was instrumental in saving God's people.

Though we may not find ourselves in such an extreme position, we still take hold of Jesus' promise:

> Everyone who acknowledges me before men, I also will acknowledge before my Father who is in heaven.
> **Matthew 10:32**

Esther ultimately points to Jesus. Christ is the ultimate intercessor for His people. He prayed for your protection from the evil one, and He now stands at the throne in heaven, identifying with you as part of His family.

You have nothing to fear. Jesus has put you where you are "'for such a time as this'" (Esth. 4:14) to continue His mission of taking His truth into the world so that others might believe and be saved.

Personal Study 2

PROVIDENCE AND RESPONSIBILITY

The book of Esther holds together two truths in Scripture that are challenging to wrap our minds around: God's providence and human responsibility.

How have you wrestled with the tension between providence and responsibility?

Why did you wrestle with understanding how one or both of those realities were true?

When has God's providence been an important truth with practical implications as to what you should do, not do, or how you should cope with a situation?

When have you found human responsibility to be an important truth with practical implications as to what you should do, not do, or how you should cope with a situation?

We see a healthy tension of both providence and responsibility expressed in Mordecai's question to Esther:

> Who knows whether you have not come to the kingdom for
> such a time as this?
> **Esther 4:14**

It is easy to discern the human responsibility side. It is harder to discern God's providence, especially when God is not mentioned once in the entire book. But consider what scholar David M. Howard, Jr. has to say on the matter:

> The best solution to God's absence from the book, however, would seem to be that the author is being intentionally vague about God's presence in events. Time and again the author seems to come close to mentioning God, only to veer away abruptly.[1]

We can perceive the vagueness in Mordecai's own words in both the question and his previous statement: "If you keep silent at this time, relief and deliverance will rise for the Jews from another place" (Esth. 4:14). Mordecai did not believe in chance or fate. He was a Jew worshiping a God who remained faithful to His covenant promises. So why not just come out and say it?

Howard continues:

> By doing this, the author seems to be affirming, on the one hand, that God indeed is involved with His people (providence) and, on the other hand, that perceiving this involvement is sometimes difficult (God's hiddenness). While the author and his readers know (rationally) that God is always present and in control, the experiences of life show that the specific manifestations of His presence are not always so clear.[2]

Without a clear calling from God as received by Adam and Abraham and Moses and Joshua, Esther determined her course of action by evaluating her position and the need of the people. In essence, she was embodying God's promise and purpose in the Abrahamic covenant (see Gen. 12:1-3) — she was blessed with the title of queen so that she might be a blessing to her people in peril.

What positions of influence has God placed you in?

What needs are around you that may be met through your position?

How has God seemed silent in areas of your life—maybe even the opportunities to meet needs and influence a situation for good?

The "hiddenness" of God also emphasizes the importance of prayer. Consider the request Esther made of Mordecai before she approached the king:

> Go, gather all the Jews to be found in Susa, and hold a fast
> on my behalf, and do not eat or drink for three days, night or day. I
> and my young women will also fast as you do. Then I will go to
> the king, though it is against the law, and if I perish, I perish.
> **Esther 4:16**

Fasting would have certainly involved prayer (another veering off by the author of Esther). It is interesting that this is the first mention of fasting (and by extension, prayer) in the book. It comes in response to the realization that she was providentially led to this position within the kingdom "for such a time as this." It comes in response to realizing that God had been with her and would use her to do something extraordinary.

When was the last time you got the sense that God had uniquely positioned you to bring about some change?

How was prayer (or even fasting) involved as you processed through your engagement in the situation?

Perhaps for the first time you are hearing God speak directly to you through Mordecai's question: "Who knows whether you have not come to the kingdom for such a time as this?" (Esth. 4:14).

We can risk losing whatever position we hold for the sake of others because, unlike Mordecai, we do not have to speculate about "relief and deliverance." We know it has already come through Jesus Christ, who freely gave up His heavenly palace (see Phil. 2:6-11) and perished to save us. We are free to risk for His kingdom because we know our future is secure in Him. All we have to do is acknowledge our opportunity.

1. David M. Howard Jr., *An Introduction to the Old Testament Historical Books* (Chicago: Moody Publishers, 1993), 375.
2. Ibid.

LEADER GUIDES

Opening and Closing Any Group Session

Always try to engage each person at the beginning of a group session. Once a person speaks, even if only answering a generic question, he or she is more likely to speak up later about more personal matters.

Begin each session by reviewing the previous week. (Suggested questions have been provided for each session.) This provides context for the new session and opportunities for individuals to share relevant experiences, application, or things learned during the time between meeting together. Then set up the theme of the study to prepare personal expectations.

Always open and close your time together with prayer, recognizing that only the Holy Spirit provides understanding and transformation in our lives. (Prayer suggestions provided in each session help focus members on Scripture, key truths, and personal application from that week's teaching.)

Remember that your goal is not just meaningful discussion, but discipleship.

Session 1: Adam

Summary statements help clarify key teaching points and provide direction for the questions that follow. (You will do this several times.)

Always keep God's Word central in discussion—ultimately we want to hear what He says. Asking someone to read Scripture can engage more people.

How does this affect your view of God? Of yourself? Of others?

What comes to mind when you think of God's character?

What about God's character is most meaningful to you?

Which parts of God's character are hardest for you to reflect? Why?

Where do you see chaos in the world? In your own life?

How do you seek to bring order out of chaos in these areas of life?
In your work? In your home?

How does knowing that God made you a steward of His creation
transform the way you approach relationships and responsibilities?

Personalized questions like these provide an entry point for discussion that
anybody can answer, regardless of previous biblical knowledge. Be aware of
any responses here about what someone has "learned" about God that are
unbiblical, but affirm attempts to grow in understanding. These questions
also provide insight into levels of spiritual maturity or life circumstances.

How did the serpent tempt Eve?

This is an example of a comprehension question. Ask these types of questions
after reading Scripture to ensure that people are recognizing specific details.

What can you learn from Adam and Eve's passivity toward sin?

**Temptation is always a lie. What are some specific examples of how
temptation promises something extraordinary apart from God?**

These are examples of questions that help people recognize the broader
implications of Scripture. By identifying specific truths like "passivity toward
sin" and "temptation is always a lie," you also provide subtle moments of
teaching and direction for responses without prescribing answers.

**What does (Genesis 3:7-13) reveal about God? About the consequences
of sin?**

These questions help group members summarize the big picture of the
session's teaching, pointing them back to God's Word for direction.

What are some things we use to try to hide from God and cover our own sin? What excuses do we make for sin?

What's an example of a sin of omission?

In which of your relationships or responsibilities are you prone to passivity? How can you be more vigilant and proactive?

Describe a way God has pursued you in a place or season when you weren't looking for Him.

What evidence of God's provision do you see? How is this provision evidence of His grace and love toward you?

Concluding your discussion time with personal application questions is important. This helps people walk away with tangible action steps for how truth affects their daily lives. Sharing personal experiences is also a great way for getting to know one another and allows people to be encouraged.

What else has been challenging, encouraging, or insightful from today's study of Adam?

Before you pray, asking for final input or questions from group members provides an opportunity for people to share or ask things that may not have been considered during discussion. This creates an environment of openness and shared ownership of your time as a group, valuing everyone's input.

Session 2: Abraham

What are some ways that you can relate to Abraham?

This type of question helps people move past some of the challenges they may have in seeing people in the Bible as real people. This helps open the door to greater confidence in applying truth from Abraham's (or any) story.

When you sense God calling you to do something, which of these three avoidance responses comes most naturally for you?

Why do we sometimes try to avoid God's call in our lives?

Like the opening question, these types of subjective questions allow people to enter discussion with (essentially) no right or wrong answer since it is a matter of identification, confession, or personal explanation. (You've also provided a summary statement from the teaching to emphasize key teaching points.)

Use this as an opportunity to remind group members that there are no "correct" answers for questions like these. You may even encourage group members to offer other responses that reflect their experience more closely.

What does this passage reveal about God? About Abraham?

This type of question encourages people to process Scripture at a level slightly deeper than basic comprehension, moving from head knowledge to understanding the heart of God and of a man to whom they can relate.

What have been some of the more challenging things you've had to leave behind to follow God?

This is a follow-up on the previous question. Abraham's story can be difficult for some to relate to because they have not left their hometowns (outside of college, perhaps) or their families. Answers may be more abstract than tangible. They are likely to include relationships, behaviors, or jobs. Remind people that repentance means leaving something sinful, but also may include not leaving something good if God calls us to do so. The emphasis here is for God to be our ultimate desire, even over good and "precious" things.

How has God's call in your life exposed areas of pride in your heart?

When was the last time following God meant walking into uncertainty?

When you've sensed God calling you to act without knowing all the details, how have you found the strength to obey?

These questions will allow group members an opportunity to share personal stories as well as acknowledge and reflect on the challenges they've faced to follow God. Sharing personal struggles helps the person sharing and also the people in the group know that they are not alone in their struggles and can provide encouragement to recognizing God's grace.

These types of questions also provide the group members (including leaders) an opportunity to see how others have processed (and progressed in) their walk with God.

How have you seen believers use their positions of influence or material resources to bless the people and families in their communities?

This question is observation that begins moving people toward personal application. This question will allow group members an opportunity to share personal stories as well as acknowledge and reflect on "the cloud of witnesses" (Hebrews 12:1) within the church.

What are some tangible blessings God has given to you?

This is a follow up to the previous question that takes the next step toward application by identifying God's goodness and beginning to recognize how those blessings are instruments for us to engage in God's mission.

What would it look like for you to be a blessing in your home? Your neighborhood? Your workplace?

This is an application question encouraging people to envision joining God's redemptive mission through their given spheres of influence. It does not ask for a specific commitment, but suggests action steps with an emphasis on a change in perspective. Though this question can lead to a call to action, worldview and values are equally as important application steps as behavior.

Session 3: Moses

When have you tried to fix a broken situation but ended up only adding to the brokenness?

How does that past experience currently play into how you engage broken situations?

Ask open-ended questions like "when have you ..." or "how does ..." that suggest common experiences and asks for people to share personal stories. Sometimes you may choose to ask a "yes" or "no" question like "have you ever ..." to engage people with a simple answer. In that case, invite people who are willing to elaborate on their responses

The goal here is for group members to discover a point of connection between Moses' story and their own. Storytelling is a great way for growing as a group. This question creates an environment for sharing relative to the text.

The follow-up question is intended to help group members consider how they are hesitant to address the brokenness, identifying a significant obstacle to their growth, or how they have learned from the experience, growing in maturity to have healthier perspectives and relationships.

What does God's appearance in the wilderness reveal about God?

Why do you think God chose to meet Moses in the wilderness?

Why do you think Moses doubted despite the signs God gave him?

The intent here is to get people in the habit of reading Scripture at a deeper level, getting to know God through His Word.

What are some things God has used to get your attention?

This question will allow group members an opportunity to share personal stories as well as acknowledge and reflect on the different ways God has spoken to them. Use questions like this as an opportunity to remind group members that there are no "correct" answers for most discussion questions.

> **How does it make you feel to know that God blessed someone who was doubtful with such a close relationship?**
>
> **How do you know when you are trying to do God's work in your own strength?**
>
> **What do you think is at the root of your attempts to act out of your own strength?**
>
> **When are you most prone to frustration and doubt?**
>
> **What do you think it looks like to invite God into your frustration?**
>
> **Where in Moses' story can you find confidence that God will treat you with compassion?**

This series of application questions helps people connect Moses' story to their own. A person may recognize specific action steps, but this week is largely focused on our internal posture before God. Remember that discipleship is about helping a person grow in maturity, not just increasing a person's knowledge. Emotive transformation is equally important as cognitive, as long as both are rooted in biblical truth.

Session 4: Joshua

> **Have you ever been in a situation that needed a leader?**
>
> **In those situations do you tend to jump in right away or wait for someone else to take charge?**

This is an example of asking for a simple yes/no response to engage people early in conversation and to help them begin connecting with Scripture on a personal level. The follow-up question opens up deeper discussion.

> When have you felt like you were in the shadow of someone else—someone who was well-known, well-liked, talented, or successful?

This question helps people relate Joshua's situation to their own. This also allows people to relate to one another on a personal level.

> What stands out to you about Joshua and Caleb's reaction?

> Of these three descriptions, which one grabs your attention the most? Why?

> What do those phrases mean to you?

> How do they encourage or challenge you?

The goal of this question is for more personal engagement by group members in the overall topic of leadership and active faith.

This question asks group members to evaluate some key principles that Darrin expressed in this week's video. The goal is to gauge the reaction of the group members to a way of thinking that may be new to them.

> What are some examples of risks that you or people you know have taken as a result of following Jesus? What is the relationship between risk and prayer?

> When have you faced a risky step of faith and needed the support and encouragement of close friends and family?

> How did your community of friends and family create courage to help you face a situation?

This final series of application questions help people synthesize what they know about risk and prayer from personal experience and their understanding of the Bible so they might see how to grow in their own risk-taking. The hope is that members will be able to articulate how they are helped by being a part of strong communities (like this group). Emphasize the need to encourage one another and hold each other accountable as a community.

Session 5: Job

When you see or experience suffering, what is your default response? If you go back and forth between the two, what explains the shift?

The goal of this question is for group members to interact with the way Darrin identified two major responses to suffering and then consider (maybe for the first time) how to describe their own response to suffering.

Why is the humanist response "foolish" and the moralist response "worthless"?

The goal of this question is to encourage group members to use biblical language as they evaluate the major non-Christian responses to suffering.

How can your suffering help you minister to someone else?

How has someone else's empathy through similar suffering helped comfort you in your own experience? How has someone else ministered to you through their quiet presence?

When has someone's advice or explanation been hurtful rather than helpful in a time of suffering or confusion?

Have you ever sat quietly with someone suffering? How difficult was it to be silent? What challenges did you face while sitting quietly?

This series of questions invites people to see the implication of the text and to share personal stories of ministering and being ministered to in suffering.

What do you think drives us to ask why? What are we hoping to find out by asking? How would knowing why help?

This question helps people evaluate their hearts, motives, and desires. The question should encourage reflection as they process the teaching.

How would you summarize what God is doing through His response? How is this response "grace" to Job?

How does God's response encourage you in your own suffering?

How did Job's view of God change? How does this change Job's response to his own suffering?

Group members will have to closely examine the biblical text in order to summarize God's response to Job. The follow-up questions help group members connect the passage to their understanding of God's character. These questions help people come to a clear understanding of the book's message by focusing on Job 42:5-6. Since this passage is poetic rather than narrative, the goal of the questions is to have group members work through rephrasing and drawing out the truth presented to ensure comprehension.

When have you experienced God in a different way while suffering?

This is a follow-up question asking group members to apply the biblical text to their own experience. This is designed to have group members consider past, present, and future experiences of suffering.

How might you experience God in a deeper way through your suffering?

This conclusion helps people reflect on how the book of Job can transform the way they process their own suffering. Remind everyone that God is still extraordinary even when they suffer without knowing "Why?"

Session 6: Esther

How would you summarize the plot? What were the key points?

Summarizing and retelling a story helps people identify key elements. Encourage everyone to add any other points they feel are important to understanding the story. Story is also a great way to share biblical truth with other people in opportunities for discipleship or evangelism.

On a scale of 0-10 (0 being *none* and 10 being *total*) how would you rate her influence over her situation at the beginning of the story? At the end of the story? Explain your ratings and any change.

Asking questions that include a scale (or multiple choice answers) can help people evaluate and identify concepts in new ways. Anyone can provide a numerical response. This leads to further explanation of their responses.

Do you think she did the right thing in her situation? Why or why not?

Without knowing the end of the story, what would you have done?

Questions like these invite people to identify with biblical figures, placing themselves in the same context. Considering their personal tendencies or decision making processes helps emphasize what Esther went through in wrestling with her faith without a miraculous sign or divine word from God. This is a relatable experience to most people who have never experienced God in such an extraordinary way as other figures studied previously.

What does God's willingness to use Esther to save His people say about Him?

If Mordecai believed that "relief and deliverance" would arise even if it didn't come through Esther, why did Esther risk her life?

These questions focus on reading comprehension and implications of the text.

How would you explain God's providence?

Looking back on your own life, how can you see God's hand bringing you to where you are today?

These questions draw attention back to a personal level, encouraging people to articulate and remember God's sovereignty. Both of these exercises encourage living by faith.

How is Esther's identification and mediation a picture of Jesus?

This type of question emphasizes the fact that all of Scripture points to Jesus. While the events and people studied are real, not metaphorical, God has been working in lives, accomplishing His mission, and revealing Himself throughout history as accurately recorded in the Bible.

What would it look like for you to identify as one of God's people in your home, workplace, school, or neighborhood?

How might you be in a position to see people saved?

What are some "ordinary events" that you've seen God use to bring healing in your family, your workplace, or your community?

This series of questions helps people envision possibilities in the future and identify opportunities in the present to be used by God for His mission of salvation through Jesus Christ. This opens them up for ongoing obedience and the ability to experience an extraordinary God in their ordinary lives.

As we conclude this study, what have you learned about God over the past 6 weeks? About your relationship with Him?

What has been the most practical takeaway helping you live out your faith in our extraordinary God?

Asking people to identify what they have learned and how it affects their relationship with God and daily lives emphasizes the fact that the goal is life transformation through discipleship, not simply gaining knowledge or having an interesting time of conversation. Reinforce the value of community centered around God's Word and relationships with each person in the group.

Tips for Leading a Group

PRAYERFULLY PREPARE

Prepare for each meeting by—

REVIEWING the weekly material and group questions ahead of time;

PRAYING for each person in the group.

Ask the Holy Spirit to work through you and the group discussion as you point to Jesus each week through God's Word.

MINIMIZE DISTRACTIONS

Create a comfortable environment. If group members are uncomfortable, they'll be distracted and therefore not engaged in the group experience. Plan ahead by taking into consideration—

SEATING;
TEMPERATURE;
LIGHTING;
FOOD OR DRINK;
SURROUNDING NOISE;
GENERAL CLEANLINESS (put away pets if meeting in a home).

At best, thoughtfulness and hospitality show guests and group members they're welcome and valued in whatever environment you choose to gather. At worst, people may never notice your effort, but they're also not distracted. Do everything in your ability to help people focus on what's most important: connecting with God, with the Bible, and with one another.

ENCOURAGE DISCUSSION

A good small-group experience has the following characteristics:

EVERYONE PARTICIPATES. Encourage everyone to ask questions, share responses, or read aloud.

NO ONE DOMINATES—NOT EVEN THE LEADER. Be sure that your time speaking as a leader takes up less than half of your time together as a group. Politely guide discussion if anyone dominates.

NOBODY IS RUSHED THROUGH QUESTIONS. Don't feel that a moment of silence is a bad thing. People often need time to think about their responses to questions they've just heard or to gain courage to share what God is stirring in their hearts.

INPUT IS AFFIRMED AND FOLLOWED UP. Make sure you point out something true or helpful in a response. Don't just move on. Build community with follow-up questions, asking how other people have experienced similar things or how a truth has shaped their understanding of God and the Scripture you're studying. People are less likely to speak up if they fear that you don't actually want to hear their answers or that you're looking for only a certain answer.

GOD AND HIS WORD ARE CENTRAL. Opinions and experiences can be helpful, but God has given us the Truth. Trust Scripture to be the authority and God's Spirit to work in people's lives. You can't change anyone, but God can. Continually point people to the Word and to active steps of faith.

INCLUDE OTHERS

Your goal is to foster a community in which people are welcomed just as they are but encouraged to grow spiritually. Always be aware of opportunities to—

INVITE new people to join your group;

INCLUDE any people who visit the group.

An inexpensive way to make first-time guests feel welcome or to invite someone to get involved is to give them their own copies of this Bible study book.

KEEP CONNECTING

Think of ways to connect with group members during the week. Participation during the group session is always improved when members spend time connecting with one another outside the group sessions. The more people are comfortable with and involved in one another's lives, the more they'll look forward to being together. When people move beyond being friendly to truly being friends who form a community, they come to each session eager to engage instead of merely attending. Encourage group members with thoughts, commitments, or questions from the session by connecting through—
PHONE CALLS;
EMAILS;
TEXTS;
SOCIAL MEDIA.

When possible, build deeper friendships by planning or spontaneously inviting group members to join you outside your regularly scheduled group time for—

MEALS;
FUN ACTIVITIES;
PROJECTS AROUND YOUR HOME, CHURCH, OR COMMUNITY.

Group Information

NAME   **CONTACT**

WHERE TO GO FROM HERE

We hope you enjoyed Extraordinary. If so, please share it on social media with #ExtraordinaryStudy. And now that you've completed this study, here are a few possible directions you can go for your next one.

CULTURE

HOLY SPIRIT

PRAYER

Learn to reclaim the distinctiveness of the Christian faith that sets it apart from the surrounding culture.
(6 sessions)

Go beyond the doctrines you already know to the Person Jesus wants you to know.
(8 sessions)

Achieve a better understanding and approach to prayer through the prayers of Paul.
(8 sessions)